LEARN SOLIDITY

100+ Coding Q&A

Yasin Cakal

Code of Code

CONTENTS

INTRODUCTION

Welcome to "Learn Solidity", the ultimate book for learning the ins and outs of Solidity, the most popular programming language for writing smart contracts on the Ethereum platform. This course is designed for beginners, but experienced programmers will also benefit from the advanced material covered.

Throughout this book, you will learn everything you need to know to start writing your own smart contracts on the Ethereum network. We will cover topics such as data types, functions, mappings, structs, and more. You will also learn how to deploy and interact with your smart contracts using web3.js.

In addition to learning the basics of Solidity, this book will also cover important topics such as security and testing. You will learn best practices for writing secure smart contracts and how to set up a testing environment to ensure the reliability of your contracts.

By the end of this book, you will have a solid understanding of Solidity and the skills to start building your own decentralized applications on the Ethereum platform. So join us now and take your first steps towards becoming a Solidity expert!

WHAT IS SOLIDITY?

If you're interested in the world of blockchain technology and decentralized applications, you've likely heard of Solidity – the most popular programming language for writing smart contracts on the Ethereum platform. But what exactly is Solidity, and why is it such an important tool for developers in the blockchain space?

In this article, we'll delve into the world of Solidity and explore what it is, its history, and how it's used in the development of decentralized applications.

A Brief History of Solidity

Before we dive into what Solidity is, let's take a step back and look at the history of this powerful programming language.

Solidity was first developed in 2014 by Dr. Christian Reitwiessner, a researcher at the Ethereum Foundation. The goal of Solidity was to create a programming language that was easy to learn and use, yet powerful enough to enable the creation of complex decentralized applications (also known as dApps).

Solidity was specifically designed to work with the Ethereum Virtual Machine (EVM), a runtime environment that executes smart contracts on the Ethereum network. With Solidity, developers can write smart contracts that run on the EVM, allowing them to build decentralized applications that can be deployed on the Ethereum network.

What is Solidity?

Now that we have a brief understanding of the history of Solidity, let's dive into what it is and how it's used.

In its simplest form, Solidity is a programming language for writing smart contracts. Smart contracts are self-executing contracts with the terms of the agreement between buyer and seller being directly written into lines of code. The code and the agreements contained therein are stored and replicated on the blockchain network.

Solidity is a high-level, contract-oriented programming language, meaning it was designed specifically for writing smart contracts. It is inspired by languages such as C++, Python, and JavaScript, making it relatively easy to learn for developers who are familiar with these languages.

One of the key features of Solidity is its support for inheritance, which allows developers to create reusable code. This makes it easier to build complex decentralized applications, as developers can reuse code from previous contracts rather than having to start from scratch each time.

Solidity is a statically-typed language, which means that variables must be declared with a specific type (such as string, integer, or boolean). This helps to prevent errors in the code, as the compiler will catch any attempts to assign a value to a variable that is of the wrong type.

How is Solidity Used?

As we mentioned earlier, Solidity is used to write smart contracts that run on the Ethereum Virtual Machine (EVM). These smart contracts can be deployed on the Ethereum network, where they can be accessed and executed by anyone with an Ethereum wallet.

Solidity is most commonly used to build decentralized applications, or dApps. These are applications that run on a decentralized network (such as the Ethereum blockchain) rather than on a single server or computer.

Decentralized applications have many benefits, including increased security (since they are not controlled by a single entity), transparency (since the code is open source and visible to all), and decentralization (since they run on a distributed network).

Some examples of decentralized applications that have been built using Solidity include:

- Cryptocurrency exchanges
- Supply chain management systems
- Voting systems
- Prediction markets
- Identity verification systems

Conclusion

In conclusion, Solidity is a powerful programming language that is specifically designed for writing smart contracts on the Ethereum platform. It is easy to learn and use, yet powerful enough to enable the creation of complex decentralized applications. With its support for inheritance and statically-typed variables, Solidity makes it easier for developers to write reliable and secure smart contracts.

Since its inception in 2014, Solidity has become the go-to language for building decentralized applications on the Ethereum platform. As the use of blockchain technology and decentralized applications continues to grow, it's likely that Solidity will only become more important in the world of software development.

If you're interested in learning Solidity and getting started with decentralized application development, be sure to check out our online course "Learn Solidity". In this course, you'll learn everything you need to know to start building your own dApps on the Ethereum network.

So why wait? Start learning Solidity today and join the growing community of developers building the decentralized future!

Exercises

To review these concepts, we will go through a series of exercises designed to test your understanding and apply what you have learned.

What is the purpose of Solidity?
Who developed Solidity and when was it developed?
What is a key feature of Solidity?
Is Solidity a statically-typed language or a dynamically-typed language?
Give an example of a decentralized application that has been built using Solidity.

Solutions

What is the purpose of Solidity?
The purpose of Solidity is to create a programming language that is easy to learn and use, yet powerful enough to enable the creation of complex decentralized applications (dApps) on the Ethereum platform.

Who developed Solidity and when was it developed?
Solidity was developed in 2014 by Dr. Christian Reitwiessner, a researcher at the Ethereum Foundation.

What is a key feature of Solidity?
One of the key features of Solidity is its support for inheritance, which allows developers to create reusable code.

Is Solidity a statically-typed language or a dynamically-typed language?
Solidity is a statically-typed language.

Give an example of a decentralized application that has been built using Solidity.
An example of a decentralized application that has been built using Solidity is a cryptocurrency exchange.

HISTORY OF SOLIDITY

If you're interested in the world of blockchain technology and decentralized applications, chances are you've heard of Solidity – the most popular programming language for writing smart contracts on the Ethereum platform. But how did Solidity come to be the go-to language for blockchain developers? In this article, we'll delve into the history of Solidity and explore how it has evolved over the years.

The Origins of Solidity

Solidity was first developed in 2014 by Dr. Christian Reitwiessner, a researcher at the Ethereum Foundation. The goal of Solidity was to create a programming language that was easy to learn and use, yet powerful enough to enable the creation of complex decentralized applications (also known as dApps).

Solidity was specifically designed to work with the Ethereum Virtual Machine (EVM), a runtime environment that executes smart contracts on the Ethereum network. With Solidity, developers could write smart contracts that would run on the EVM, allowing them to build decentralized applications that could be deployed on the Ethereum network.

The Early Years of Solidity

In the early years of its development, Solidity was primarily used by a small community of developers who were interested in building decentralized applications on the Ethereum platform. The language was still in its infancy, and there were relatively few resources available for developers who wanted to learn it.

Despite this, Solidity quickly gained traction among developers due to its simplicity and power. It was easy to learn for developers who were familiar with languages such as C++, Python, and JavaScript, and it provided a wide range of features that made it well-suited for building decentralized applications.

The Rise of Solidity

As the Ethereum platform and decentralized applications gained popularity, so too did Solidity. More and more developers began using the language to build dApps, and a growing number of resources became available for those who wanted to learn it.

In 2016, Solidity reached a major milestone with the release of version 0.4.0. This version introduced a number of significant updates, including support for the new Ethereum network protocol (EIP-150), as well as a number of other enhancements and bug fixes.

The Solidity of Today

Today, Solidity is the most popular programming language for writing smart contracts on the Ethereum platform. It is used by thousands of developers around the world to build decentralized applications of all kinds, from cryptocurrency exchanges to voting systems to supply chain management systems.

Solidity has come a long way since its early days in 2014. It has evolved significantly, with new versions being released on a regular basis that introduce new features and improvements. Today, it is a mature and well-established language that is here to stay.

Conclusion

In conclusion, Solidity is a powerful programming language that has come a long way since its inception in 2014. From its early days as a language used by a small community of developers, it has evolved into the most popular language for writing smart contracts on the Ethereum platform. Today, it is used by thousands of developers around the world to build decentralized applications of all kinds.

Exercises

To review these concepts, we will go through a series of exercises designed to test your understanding and apply what you have learned.

Find and describe at least 3 major updates or changes that have been made to Solidity since its inception.

Find and describe an example of a Solidity contract that has been exploited or had a security vulnerability.

What major update was released in version 0.4.0 of Solidity?

Find and describe a real-world application or project that is using Solidity as its primary programming language.

Is Solidity a mature and well-established language?

Solutions

Find and describe at least 3 major updates or changes that have been made to Solidity since its inception.

Some major updates to Solidity include:

- The 0.5.0 release in 2019, which introduced support for the new experimental ABI encoding, as well as breaking changes to the syntax and standard library.
- The 0.6.0 release in 2020, which introduced support for the new Ethereum 2.0 Beacon Chain and introduced a new experimental syntax for declaring structs.
- The 0.7.0 release in 2021, which introduced a new experimental type system, improved error messages, and added support for the Ethereum Virtual Machine (EVM) optimizer.

Find and describe an example of a Solidity contract that has been exploited or had a security vulnerability.

One example of a Solidity contract that had a security vulnerability is the Parity Wallet contract. In 2017, a hacker was able to exploit a vulnerability in the contract's code, allowing them to steal over 150,000 ether (worth millions of dollars at the time). The vulnerability was caused by a mistake in the contract's initialization code, which allowed the hacker to gain access to the contract's owner's keys and steal their ether.

What major update was released in version 0.4.0 of Solidity?
In version 0.4.0 of Solidity, support for the new Ethereum network protocol (EIP-150) was introduced, as well as a number of other enhancements and bug fixes.

Find and describe a real-world application or project that is using Solidity as its primary programming language.
One real-world application that is using Solidity is the Augur prediction market platform. Augur is a decentralized platform that allows users to create and participate in prediction markets on a wide range of topics. It uses Solidity to write the smart contracts that are used to facilitate the creation and operation of these markets, as well as to handle the automatic payout of winnings to users.

Is Solidity a mature and well-established language?
Yes, Solidity is a mature and well-established language. It has evolved significantly since its early days, with new versions being released on a regular basis that introduce new features and improvements.

SETTING UP A DEVELOPMENT ENVIRONMENT

If you're ready to start learning Solidity and building decentralized applications (dApps) on the Ethereum platform, the first step is setting up a development environment. In this article, we'll walk you through the process of setting up a Solidity development environment, step by step.

Step 1: Install Node.js and npm

The first thing you'll need to do is install Node.js and npm (the Node.js package manager). Node.js is a JavaScript runtime that allows you to run JavaScript on the server-side, and npm is a package manager that makes it easy to install and manage dependencies.

To install Node.js and npm, go to the Node.js website (https://nodejs.org/) and download the latest version. Follow the installation instructions, and once the installation is complete, you should be able to open a terminal window and type "node -v" to check the version of Node.js that you have installed. You should see something like "v12.18.3" (the exact version may vary).

Step 2: Install Truffle

Next, you'll need to install Truffle, a popular development framework for Ethereum. Truffle makes it easy to write, test, and deploy Solidity contracts, and it comes with a variety of tools and libraries that make it easier to develop dApps.

To install Truffle, open a terminal window and type the following command:

```
npm install -g truffle
```

This will install Truffle globally on your system, which means you'll be able to use it from any project.

Step 3: Install a Solidity Compiler

In order to compile Solidity code, you'll need to install a Solidity compiler. There are several Solidity compilers available, but the most popular is Remix, which is a browser-based compiler that is easy to use and gets the job done.

To use Remix, simply go to the Remix website (https://remix.ethereum.org/) and start writing and compiling Solidity code in your browser.

Alternatively, if you prefer to use a command-line compiler, you can install the Solidity compiler by running the following command:

```
npm install -g solc
```

Step 4: Install an Ethereum Client

Finally, you'll need to install an Ethereum client in order to interact with the Ethereum network and deploy your dApps. There are several Ethereum clients available, but the most popular is Geth, which is written in Go.

To install Geth, visit the Geth website (https://geth.ethereum.org/) and follow the installation instructions. Once Geth is installed, you'll be able to use it to connect to the Ethereum network and deploy your dApps.

Conclusion

In conclusion, setting up a Solidity development environment is a straightforward process that requires the installation of a few key tools. By following the steps outlined in this article, you'll be well on your way to building your own dApps on the Ethereum platform.

Exercises

To review these concepts, we will go through a series of exercises designed to test your understanding and apply what you have learned.

What is Node.js?
What is npm?
What is Truffle?
What is Remix?
What is Geth?

Solutions

What is Node.js?
Node.js is a JavaScript runtime that allows you to run JavaScript on the server-side.

What is npm?
npm (the Node.js package manager) is a package manager that makes it easy to install and manage dependencies.

What is Truffle?
Truffle is a popular development framework for Ethereum that makes it easy to write, test, and deploy Solidity contracts.

What is Remix?
Remix is a browser-based Solidity compiler that is easy to use and gets the job done.

What is Geth?
Geth is an Ethereum client written in Go that is used to connect to the Ethereum network and deploy dApps.

VARIABLES

As a Solidity developer, it's important to have a strong understanding of variables – one of the most fundamental concepts in programming. In this article, we'll take a closer look at variables in Solidity, including how to declare them, the different types of variables available, and how to use them in your code.

What are Variables?

In programming, a variable is a named location in memory where a value can be stored and accessed. Variables are used to store data that can be used and manipulated by the program.

In Solidity, variables are declared using the "var" keyword, followed by the variable name and the type of data that the variable will hold. For example:

```
var myVariable uint256;
```

This code declares a variable called "myVariable" that can hold an unsigned integer (uint) of 256 bits.

Types of Variables in Solidity

Solidity supports a wide range of variable types, including integers, booleans, and strings. Here are some of the most commonly used variable types in Solidity:

- uint: Unsigned integer (positive whole number)
- int: Signed integer (positive or negative whole number)
- bool: Boolean (true or false)
- string: String (sequence of characters)

In addition to these basic types, Solidity also supports arrays, mappings, and structs, which allow you to store more complex data structures.

Arrays are used to store a list of items of the same type. For example:

```
uint[] myArray;
```

This code declares an array of unsigned integers called "myArray".

Mappings are used to store key-value pairs, similar to a dictionary in other languages. For example:

```
mapping(address => uint) balances;
```

This code declares a mapping called "balances" that maps addresses (the keys) to unsigned integers (the values).

Structs are used to define custom data types that can be composed of several different types. For example:

```
struct User {
  string name;
  uint age;
}
```

This code declares a struct called "User" that has two fields: a string called "name" and an unsigned integer called "age".

Using Variables in Solidity

Once you've declared a variable, you can use it in your code by referencing its name. For example:

```
function setAge(uint newAge) public {
  age = newAge;
}
```

This code defines a function called "setAge" that takes an unsigned integer as an argument and assigns it to the "age" variable.

You can also access the value of a variable by referencing its name. For example:

```
function getAge() public view returns (uint) {
  return age;
}
```

This code defines a function called "getAge" that returns the value of the "age" variable.

Conclusion

In conclusion, variables are a fundamental concept in programming that are used to store and manipulate data in a program. In Solidity, variables are declared using the "var" keyword and can be of several different types, including integers, booleans, and strings. Once a variable has been declared, it can be used and accessed in your code by referencing its name. Understanding how to use variables is essential for building effective Solidity contracts and decentralized applications.

Exercises

To review these concepts, we will go through a series of exercises designed to test your understanding and apply what you have learned.

What is a variable in programming?
How are variables declared in Solidity?
What is an array in Solidity?
What is a mapping in Solidity?
What is a struct in Solidity?

Solutions

What is a variable in programming?

In programming, a variable is a named location in memory where a value can be stored and accessed.

How are variables declared in Solidity?

In Solidity, variables are declared using the "var" keyword, followed by the variable name and the type of data that the variable will hold. For example: "var myVariable uint256;".

What is an array in Solidity?

An array in Solidity is used to store a list of items of the same type. For example: "uint[] myArray;".

What is a mapping in Solidity?

A mapping in Solidity is used to store key-value pairs, similar to a dictionary in other languages. For example: "mapping(address => uint) balances;".

What is a struct in Solidity?

A struct in Solidity is used to define a custom data type that can be composed of several different types. For example: "struct User { string name; uint age; }".

DATA TYPES

In Solidity, data types are used to specify the type of data that a variable or constant can hold. Understanding the different data types available in Solidity is essential for building effective contracts and decentralized applications. In this article, we'll take a closer look at the various data types available in Solidity and how they can be used in your code.

Numeric Data Types

Solidity offers a range of numeric data types, including integers, fixed-point numbers, and unsigned integers. Here are some of the most commonly used numeric data types in Solidity:

- uint: Unsigned integer (positive whole number)
- int: Signed integer (positive or negative whole number)
- uint8 to uint256: Unsigned integer of 8 to 256 bits
- int8 to int256: Signed integer of 8 to 256 bits
- fixed: Fixed-point number
- fixed8x8 to fixed256x256: Fixed-point number with 8 to 256 bits before and after the decimal point

For example, the following code declares an unsigned integer called "myNumber" that can hold a value between 0 and 2^256-1:

```
uint256 myNumber;
```

Boolean Data Type

Solidity also offers a boolean data type, which can hold the values true or false. The boolean data type is commonly used to represent the results of logical operations or to control the flow of a program.

For example, the following code declares a boolean called "isValid" and sets its value to true:

```
bool isValid = true;
```

String Data Type

In Solidity, the string data type is used to represent a sequence of characters. Strings are commonly used to store text data, such as names, addresses, and descriptions.

To declare a string variable in Solidity, use the "string" keyword followed by the variable name. For example:

```
string myString;
```

This code declares a string called "myString".

Arrays

In Solidity, arrays are used to store a list of items of the same type. Arrays can be of any data type, including integers, booleans, and strings.

To declare an array in Solidity, use the data type of the items followed by square brackets and the variable name. For example:

```
uint[] myArray;
```

This code declares an array of unsigned integers called "myArray".

Mappings

Mappings in Solidity are used to store key-value pairs, similar to a dictionary in other languages. Mappings can be of any data type, and the keys can be of any data type that is hashable (able to be converted to a unique fixed-size value).

To declare a mapping in Solidity, use the "mapping" keyword followed by the key data type, an arrow, and the value data type, and then the variable name. For example:

```
mapping(address => uint) balances;
```

This code declares a mapping called "balances" that maps addresses (the keys) to unsigned integers (the values).

Structs

Structs in Solidity are used to define custom data types that can be composed of several different types. Structs are useful for organizing and grouping related data together.

To declare a struct in Solidity, use the "struct" keyword followed by the struct name and a set of curly braces containing the fields of the struct. For example:

```
struct User {
  string name;
  uint age;
}
```

This code declares a struct called "User" that has two fields: a string called "name" and an unsigned integer called "age".

Conclusion

In conclusion, data types are an important concept in Solidity that are used to specify the type of data that a variable or constant can hold. Solidity offers a range of data types, including numeric types, booleans, strings, arrays, mappings, and structs. Understanding the different data types available in Solidity and how to use them is essential for building effective contracts and decentralized applications.

Exercises

To review these concepts, we will go through a series of exercises designed to test your understanding and apply what you have learned.

What is a numeric data type?
What is the boolean data type used for in Solidity?
Write a Solidity function that takes in an array of integers as an argument and returns the sum of all the elements in the array.
Write a Solidity function that takes in a struct as an argument and returns the struct's values as a string.
Write a Solidity function that takes in an array of structs as an argument and returns the sum of all the ages of the structs in the array.

Solutions

What is a numeric data type?
A numeric data type is a data type that represents a number. Solidity offers several numeric data types, including integers, fixed-point numbers, and unsigned integers.

What is the boolean data type used for in Solidity?
The boolean data type in Solidity is used to represent the values true or false. It is commonly used to represent the results of logical operations or to control the flow of a program.

Write a Solidity function that takes in an array of integers as an argument and returns the sum of all the elements in the array.

```solidity
function findSum(int[] arr) public pure returns (int) {
    int sum = 0;
    for (uint i = 0; i < arr.length; i++) {
        sum += arr[i];
    }
    return sum;
}
```

Write a Solidity function that takes in a struct as an argument and returns the struct's values as a string.

```solidity
function convertStructToString(StructType myStruct) public pure returns (string memory) {
    return "Name: " + myStruct.name + ", Age: " + myStruct.age + ", Address: " + myStruct.address;
}
```

Write a Solidity function that takes in an array of structs as an argument and returns the sum of all the ages of the structs in the array.

```solidity
function findSumOfStructAges(StructType[] arr) public pure returns (uint) {
    uint sum = 0;
```

```
for (uint i = 0; i < arr.length; i++) {
  sum += arr[i].age;
}
return sum;
}
```

FUNCTIONS

In Solidity, functions are blocks of code that can be called and executed at any time. Functions are a key concept in programming and are used to organize and reuse code, making it easier to develop and maintain complex programs. In this article, we'll take a closer look at functions in Solidity, including how to define and call functions, and how to use function parameters and return values.

Defining Functions

In Solidity, functions are defined using the "function" keyword followed by the function name and a set of parentheses. The function name should be a descriptive name that reflects the purpose of the function.

For example, the following code defines a function called "incrementCounter" that increments a counter by one:

```
function incrementCounter() public {
  counter++;
}
```

Function Parameters

Functions can accept input in the form of function parameters. Function parameters are specified in the parentheses after the function name, and they allow the function to accept and process different values each time it is called.

For example, the following code defines a function called "addNumbers" that takes two integers as parameters and returns their sum:

```
function addNumbers(int a, int b) public returns (int) {
  return a + b;
}
```

Function Return Values

In Solidity, functions can return a value using the "return" keyword. Return values allow a function to pass data back to the calling code, allowing it to be used or processed further.

To specify the data type of the return value, use the "returns" keyword followed by the data type in parentheses after the function definition. For example:

```
function getAge() public returns (uint) {
```

```
return age;
```

```
}
```

This code defines a function called "getAge" that returns an unsigned integer (uint).

Calling Functions

To call a function in Solidity, use the function name followed by a set of parentheses and any necessary arguments. For example:

```
incrementCounter();
```

This code calls the "incrementCounter" function.

If the function takes parameters, you can pass them in the parentheses. For example:

```
int result = addNumbers(3, 4);
```

This code calls the "addNumbers" function with the arguments 3 and 4, and assigns the returned value to the "result" variable.

Conclusion

In conclusion, functions are a key concept in programming that are used to organize and reuse code. In Solidity, functions are defined using the "function" keyword, and they can accept parameters and return values. Functions can be called and executed at any time, allowing you to reuse code and make your contracts and decentralized applications more efficient and maintainable.

Exercises

To review these concepts, we will go through a series of exercises designed to test your understanding and apply what you have learned.

What is a function in programming?
How are functions defined in Solidity?
What are function parameters?
How do you specify the data type of a function's return value in Solidity?
How do you call a function in Solidity?

Solutions

What is a function in programming?
In programming, a function is a block of code that can be called and executed at any time. Functions are used to organize and reuse code, making it easier to develop and maintain complex programs.

How are functions defined in Solidity?
In Solidity, functions are defined using the "function" keyword followed by the function name and a set of parentheses. For example: "function incrementCounter() public { counter++; }".

What are function parameters?

Function parameters are specified in the parentheses after the function name and allow the function to accept and process different values each time it is called.

How do you specify the data type of a function's return value in Solidity?
To specify the data type of a function's return value in Solidity, use the "returns" keyword followed by the data type in parentheses after the function definition. For example: "function getAge() public returns (uint) { return age; }".

How do you call a function in Solidity?
To call a function in Solidity, use the function name followed by a set of parentheses and any necessary arguments. For example: "incrementCounter();". If the function takes parameters, you can pass them in the parentheses. For example: "int result = addNumbers(3, 4);".

MODIFIERS

In Solidity, modifiers are used to add additional behavior or conditions to functions. Modifiers are a key concept in programming that allow you to add flexibility and customization to your code. In this article, we'll take a closer look at modifiers in Solidity, including how to define and use them, and how they can be combined with other Solidity features to create more powerful contracts and decentralized applications.

Defining Modifiers

In Solidity, modifiers are defined using the "modifier" keyword followed by the modifier name and a set of curly braces containing the code that the modifier will execute. Modifiers do not have a return value and are not self-executing; they must be applied to a function in order to take effect.

For example, the following code defines a modifier called "onlyOwner" that allows only the contract owner to execute the function it is applied to:

```
modifier onlyOwner {
  require(msg.sender == owner);
  _;
}
```

This modifier uses the "require" function to check that the sender of the message (msg.sender) is the owner of the contract. If the check passes, the code continues to execute; if it fails, the function execution is halted and an exception is thrown.

The ";" line in the modifier code is a placeholder for the code that the modifier will be applied to. When the modifier is applied to a function, the code in the function will be inserted in place of the ";".

Applying Modifiers

To apply a modifier to a function in Solidity, use the "modifier" keyword followed by the modifier name in the function definition. For example:

```
function setAge(uint newAge) public onlyOwner {
  age = newAge;
}
```

This code defines a function called "setAge" that accepts an unsigned integer as a parameter and sets the "age" variable to the new value. The "onlyOwner" modifier is applied to the function, meaning that only the contract owner will be be able to execute it.

Combining Modifiers

In Solidity, you can combine multiple modifiers in a single function definition by separating them with commas. This allows you to add multiple layers of behavior or conditions to a function.

For example, the following code defines a function called "transfer" that combines the "onlyOwner" and "notPaused" modifiers:

```
function transfer(address recipient, uint amount) public onlyOwner, notPaused {
    require(recipient != address(0));
    require(balance >= amount);
    recipient.transfer(amount);
    balance -= amount;
}
```

This function will only be able to be executed if the contract is not paused and if the sender of the message is the contract owner. Additionally, the function includes two "require" statements that check the validity of the recipient address and the available balance before executing the transfer.

Conclusion

In conclusion, modifiers are a powerful tool in Solidity that allow you to add additional behavior or conditions to functions. Modifiers are defined using the "modifier" keyword and applied to functions using the "modifier" keyword followed by the modifier name. Modifiers can be combined to create more complex and customizable functions, making your contracts and decentralized applications more powerful and flexible.

Exercises

To review these concepts, we will go through a series of exercises designed to test your understanding and apply what you have learned.

What is a modifier in Solidity?
How are modifiers defined in Solidity?
How do you apply a modifier to a function in Solidity?
Can multiple modifiers be combined in a single function definition in Solidity?
What is the "_;" line in a Solidity modifier used for?

Solutions

What is a modifier in Solidity?
In Solidity, a modifier is a block of code that is used to add additional behavior or conditions to a function. Modifiers do not have a return value and are not self-executing; they must be applied to a function in order to take effect.

How are modifiers defined in Solidity?
In Solidity, modifiers are defined using the "modifier" keyword followed by the modifier name and a

set of curly braces containing the code that the modifier will execute.

How do you apply a modifier to a function in Solidity?

To apply a modifier to a function in Solidity, use the "modifier" keyword followed by the modifier name in the function definition. For example: "function setAge(uint newAge) public onlyOwner { age = newAge; }".

Can multiple modifiers be combined in a single function definition in Solidity?

Yes, in Solidity you can combine multiple modifiers in a single function definition by separating them with commas. This allows you to add multiple layers of behavior or conditions to a function.

What is the "_;" line in a Solidity modifier used for?

In Solidity, the "_;" line in a modifier is a placeholder for the code that the modifier will be applied to. When the modifier is applied to a function, the code in the function will be inserted in place of the "_;".

MAPPINGS

In Solidity, mappings are used to store key-value pairs, similar to a dictionary in other languages. Mappings are a powerful and flexible data structure that can be used to store and retrieve data in a contract. In this article, we'll take a closer look at mappings in Solidity, including how to define and use them, and how to iterate over the keys and values in a mapping.

Defining Mappings

In Solidity, mappings are defined using the "mapping" keyword followed by the key data type, an arrow, and the value data type, and then the variable name. The key data type can be any data type that is hashable (able to be converted to a unique fixed-size value), while the value data type can be any data type.

For example, the following code defines a mapping called "balances" that maps addresses (the keys) to unsigned integers (the values):

```
mapping(address => uint) balances;
```

This mapping can be used to store the balance of each address in the contract.

Using Mappings

To access the value of a key in a mapping, use the mapping name followed by the key in square brackets. For example:

```
balances[msg.sender]++;
```

This code retrieves the value of the "msg.sender" key in the "balances" mapping and increments it by one.

To set the value of a key in a mapping, use the mapping name followed by the key in square brackets, followed by the assignment operator and the new value. For example:

```
balances[recipient] = amount;
```

This code sets the value of the "recipient" key in the "balances" mapping to the "amount" value.

Iterating Over Mapping Keys and Values

In Solidity, it is not possible to directly iterate over the keys and values in a mapping. However, it is possible to create a separate data structure (such as an array) and store the keys or values in it, and then iterate over that data structure.

For example, the following code creates an array called "accounts" and stores all of the keys (addresses) in the "balances" mapping in it:

```
address[] accounts;
function getAccounts() public {
  for (uint i = 0; i < balances.length; i++) {
    accounts.push(balances[i].key);
  }
}
```

This code defines a function called "getAccounts" that iterates over the keys in the "balances" mapping and stores them in the "accounts" array.

Conclusion

In conclusion, mappings in Solidity are a powerful and flexible data structure that can be used to store and retrieve key-value pairs. Mappings are defined using the "mapping" keyword and accessed using square brackets and the key. While it is not possible to directly iterate over the keys and values in a mapping, it is possible to create a separate data structure and store the keys or values in it, and then iterate over that data structure. Mappings are a useful tool for storing and managing data in Solidity contracts and decentralized applications.

Exercises

To review these concepts, we will go through a series of exercises designed to test your understanding and apply what you have learned.

What is a mapping in Solidity?
How are mappings defined in Solidity?
How do you access the value of a key in a mapping in Solidity?
How do you set the value of a key in a mapping in Solidity?
Can you iterate over the keys and values in a mapping in Solidity?

Solutions

What is a mapping in Solidity?
In Solidity, a mapping is a data structure that is used to store key-value pairs. Mappings are similar to a dictionary in other languages and are a useful tool for storing and managing data in contracts and decentralized applications.

How are mappings defined in Solidity?
In Solidity, mappings are defined using the "mapping" keyword followed by the key data type, an arrow, and the value data type, and then the variable name. For example: "mapping(address => uint) balances;".

How do you access the value of a key in a mapping in Solidity?
To access the value of a key in a mapping in Solidity, use the mapping name followed by the key in square brackets. For example: "balances[msg.sender]++;".

How do you set the value of a key in a mapping in Solidity?
To set the value of a key in a mapping in Solidity, use the mapping name followed by the key in square brackets, followed by the assignment operator and the new value. For example: "balances[recipient] = amount;".

Can you iterate over the keys and values in a mapping in Solidity?
In Solidity, it is not possible to directly iterate over the keys and values in a mapping. However, it is possible to create a separate data structure (such as an array) and store the keys or values in it, and then iterate over that data structure.

STRUCTS

In Solidity, structs are used to create custom data types that can store multiple variables of different types. Structs are a key concept in programming that allow you to create complex and reusable data structures, making it easier to manage and organize data in your contracts and decentralized applications. In this article, we'll take a closer look at structs in Solidity, including how to define and use them, and how to access and modify their variables.

Defining Structs

In Solidity, structs are defined using the "struct" keyword followed by the struct name and a set of curly braces containing the variables that the struct will contain. The variables in a struct can be of any data type, and multiple structs can be defined in a single contract.

For example, the following code defines a struct called "Person" that contains three variables: "name", "age", and "height":

```
struct Person {
  string name;
  uint age;
  uint height;
}
```

This struct can be used to store information about a person, such as their name, age, and height.

Creating Struct Instances

To create an instance of a struct in Solidity, use the "new" keyword followed by the struct name and a set of parentheses. For example:

```
Person p = new Person();
```

This code creates a new instance of the "Person" struct called "p".

Accessing and Modifying Struct Variables

To access or modify a variable in a struct instance, use the instance name followed by a period and the variable name. For example:

```
p.name = "Alice";
p.age = 25;
p.height = 170;
```

This code sets the "name" variable of the "p" struct instance to "Alice", the "age" variable to 25, and the "height" variable to 170.

To access the value of a struct variable, use the instance name followed by a period and the variable name. For example:

```
string name = p.name;
uint age = p.age;
uint height = p.height;
```

This code retrieves the values of the "name", "age", and "height" variables in the "p" struct instance and stores them in separate variables.

Passing Structs as Function Parameters

In Solidity, structs can be passed as function parameters in the same way as other data types. For example:

```
function setPerson(Person person) public {
person.name = "Bob";
person.age = 30;
person.height = 180;
}
```

This function defines a parameter called "person" of type "Person" and modifies its "name", "age", and "height" variables.

Conclusion

In conclusion, structs in Solidity are a useful tool for creating custom data types that can store multiple variables of different types. Structs are defined using the "struct" keyword and instances are created using the "new" keyword. Struct variables can be accessed and modified using the instance name followed by a period and the variable name. Structs can be passed as function parameters and are a useful way to manage and organize data in Solidity contracts and decentralized applications.

Exercises

To review these concepts, we will go through a series of exercises designed to test your understanding and apply what you have learned.

What is a struct in Solidity?
How are structs defined in Solidity?
How do you create an instance of a struct in Solidity?
How do you access and modify the variables in a struct instance in Solidity?
Can structs be passed as function parameters in Solidity?

Solutions

What is a struct in Solidity?

In Solidity, a struct is a custom data type that is used to store multiple variables of different types. Structs are a key concept in programming that allow you to create complex and reusable data structures, making it easier to manage and organize data in your contracts and decentralized applications.

How are structs defined in Solidity?

In Solidity, structs are defined using the "struct" keyword followed by the struct name and a set of curly braces containing the variables that the struct will contain. The variables in a struct can be of any data type, and multiple structs can be defined in a single contract.

How do you create an instance of a struct in Solidity?

To create an instance of a struct in Solidity, use the "new" keyword followed by the struct name and a set of parentheses. For example: "Person p = new Person();".

How do you access and modify the variables in a struct instance in Solidity?

To access or modify a variable in a struct instance in Solidity, use the instance name followed by a period and the variable name. For example: "p.name = "Alice";".

Can structs be passed as function parameters in Solidity?

Yes, in Solidity, structs can be passed as function parameters in the same way as other data types. For example: "function setPerson(Person person) public { … }".

ARRAYS

In Solidity, arrays are used to store collections of data of the same data type. Arrays are a key concept in programming that allow you to store and manipulate large amounts of data in an organized and efficient way. In this article, we'll take a closer look at arrays in Solidity, including how to define and use them, and how to access and modify their elements.

Defining Arrays

In Solidity, arrays are defined using the data type of the elements followed by the square brackets, and then the array name. The data type of the elements can be any data type, and the size of the array can be fixed or dynamic.

For example, the following code defines a fixed-size array of integers called "numbers" with a size of 10:

```
uint[10] numbers;
```

This array can be used to store up to 10 integer values.

To define a dynamic-size array, use the "new" keyword followed by the data type of the elements and the square brackets, and then the array name. For example:

```
uint[] dynamicNumbers;
```

This array can be used to store an unlimited number of integer values, and its size can be changed at runtime.

Accessing and Modifying Array Elements

To access or modify an element in an array, use the array name followed by the index of the element in square brackets. The index of the first element in an array is 0, and the index of the last element is the size of the array minus 1.

For example, the following code sets the first element of the "numbers" array to 10:

```
numbers[0] = 10;
```

This code sets the value of the element at index 0 in the "numbers" array to 10.

To access the value of an array element, use the array name followed by the index of the element in square brackets. For example:

```
uint firstNumber = numbers[0];
```

This code retrieves the value of the element at index 0 in the "numbers" array and stores it in the "firstNumber" variable.

Iterating Over Arrays

In Solidity, it is possible to iterate over the elements in an array using a for loop. The for loop can be used to access or modify each element in the array sequentially.

For example, the following code iterates over the "numbers" array and prints each element to the console:

```
for (uint i = 0; i < numbers.length; i++) {
  conscle.log(numbers[i]);
}
```

This code defines a for loop that iterates over the elements in the "numbers" array and prints each element to the console using the "console.log" function. The loop variable "i" is used as the index of the current element, and the "length" property of the "numbers" array is used to determine the number of elements in the array.

Multidimensional Arrays

In Solidity, it is also possible to define multidimensional arrays, which are arrays of arrays. Multidimensional arrays are useful for storing and manipulating data that has more than one dimension, such as matrices or tables.

To define a multidimensional array, use multiple sets of square brackets after the data type of the elements. For example, the following code defines a two-dimensional array of integers called "matrix" with a size of 3 rows and 4 columns:

```
uint[3][4] matrix;
```

This array can be used to store 3 rows of 4 integer values each.

To access or modify an element in a multidimensional array, use multiple sets of square brackets with the indices of the element. For example, the following code sets the value of the element at row 1, column 2 in the "matrix" array to 10:

```
matrix[1][2] = 10;
```

This code sets the value of the element at index (1, 2) in the "matrix" array to 10.

Conclusion

In conclusion, arrays in Solidity are a useful tool for storing and manipulating collections of data of the same data type. Arrays can be fixed-size or dynamic-size, and their elements can be accessed and modified using indices in square brackets. It is possible to iterate over the elements in an array using a for loop, and multidimensional arrays can be defined to store data with more than one dimension. Arrays are a key concept in programming and are a useful way to manage and organize data in Solidity contracts and decentralized applications.

What is an array in Solidity?
How are arrays defined in Solidity?
How do you access and modify the elements in an array in Solidity?
How do you iterate over the elements in an array in Solidity?
Can you define multidimensional arrays in Solidity?

Solutions

What is an array in Solidity?

In Solidity, an array is a data structure that is used to store a collection of data of the same data type. Arrays are a key concept in programming that allow you to store and manipulate large amounts of data in an organized and efficient way.

How are arrays defined in Solidity?

In Solidity, arrays are defined using the data type of the elements followed by the square brackets, and then the array name. The data type of the elements can be any data type, and the size of the array can be fixed or dynamic. To define a dynamic-size array, use the "new" keyword followed by the data type of the elements and the square brackets, and then the array name.

How do you access and modify the elements in an array in Solidity?

To access or modify an element in an array in Solidity, use the array name followed by the index of the element in square brackets. The index of the first element in an array is 0, and the index of the last element is the size of the array minus 1.

How do you iterate over the elements in an array in Solidity?

In Solidity, you can iterate over the elements in an array using a for loop. The for loop can be used to access or modify each element in the array sequentially.

Can you define multidimensional arrays in Solidity?

Yes, in Solidity, it is possible to define multidimensional arrays, which are arrays of arrays. Multidimensional arrays are useful for storing and manipulating data that has more than one dimension, such as matrices or tables. To define a multidimensional array, use multiple sets of square brackets after the data type of the elements. To access or modify an element in a multidimensional array, use multiple sets of square brackets with the indices of the element.

ENUMS

In Solidity, enums (short for enumerations) are used to create custom data types with a fixed set of values. Enums are a key concept in programming that allow you to create custom data types with a limited set of options, making it easier to manage and organize data in your contracts and decentralized applications. In this article, we'll take a closer look at enums in Solidity, including how to define and use them, and how to access and modify their values.

Defining Enums

In Solidity, enums are defined using the "enum" keyword followed by the enum name and a set of curly braces containing the values that the enum will contain. The values in an enum can be of any data type, and multiple enums can be defined in a single contract.

For example, the following code defines an enum called "Colors" that contains four values: "Red", "Green", "Blue", and "Yellow":

```
enum Colors { Red, Green, Blue, Yellow }
```

This enum can be used to store one of four possible color values.

Creating Enum Instances

To create an instance of an enum in Solidity, use the enum name followed by a period and one of the values in the enum. For example:

```
Colors c = Colors.Red;
```

This code creates a new instance of the "Colors" enum called "c" and sets its value to "Red".

Accessing and Modifying Enum Values

To access the value of an enum instance, use the instance name. For example:

```
string color = c;
```

This code retrieves the value of the "c" enum instance and stores it in the "color" variable.

To modify the value of an enum instance, use the instance name followed by an assignment operator and one of the values in the enum. For example:

```
c = Colors.Green;
```

This code sets the value of the "c" enum instance to "Green".

Comparing Enum Values

In Solidity, it is possible to compare the values of enum instances using comparison operators such as "==" (equal to) and "!=" (not equal to). For example:

```
if (c == Colors.Red) {
  console.log("The color is red.");
}
```

This code checks if the value of the "c" enum instance is equal to "Red" and, if so, prints a message to the console.

Using Enums as Function Parameters

In Solidity, enums can be passed as function parameters in the same way as other data types. For example:

```
function setColor(Colors color) public {
  c = color;
}
```

This function takes an enum instance of the "Colors" type as a parameter and sets it as the value of the "c" enum instance.

Using Enums as Mapping Keys

In Solidity, it is also possible to use enums as keys in mappings. Mappings are data structures that store key-value pairs, and they are useful for storing and accessing data efficiently.

For example, the following code defines a mapping that uses the "Colors" enum as the key and the "string" data type as the value:

```
mapping (Colors => string) colorNames;
```

This mapping can be used to store the names of colors as strings, using the values in the "Colors" enum as the keys.

To access or modify a value in a mapping, use the mapping name followed by the key in square brackets. For example:

```
colorNames[Colors.Red] = "Red";
```

This code sets the value of the "Red" key in the "colorNames" mapping to "Red".

Conclusion

In conclusion, enums in Solidity are a useful tool for creating custom data types with fixed values. Enums can be used to store and manipulate data with a limited set of options, and they can be passed as function parameters and used as mapping keys. Enums are a key concept in programming and are a useful way to manage and organize data in Solidity contracts and decentralized applications.

Exercises

To review these concepts, we will go through a series of exercises designed to test your understanding and apply what you have learned.

What is an enum in Solidity?
How are enums defined in Solidity?
How do you create an instance of an enum in Solidity?
How do you access and modify the values of enum instances in Solidity?
Can you use enums as function parameters and mapping keys in Solidity?

Solutions

What is an enum in Solidity?
In Solidity, an enum (short for enumeration) is a custom data type that contains a fixed set of values. Enums are a key concept in programming that allow you to create custom data types with a limited set of options, making it easier to manage and organize data in your contracts and decentralized applications.

How are enums defined in Solidity?
In Solidity, enums are defined using the "enum" keyword followed by the enum name and a set of curly braces containing the values that the enum will contain. The values in an enum can be of any data type, and multiple enums can be defined in a single contract.

How do you create an instance of an enum in Solidity?
To create an instance of an enum in Solidity, use the enum name followed by a period and one of the values in the enum. For example: "Colors c = Colors.Red". This code creates a new instance of the "Colors" enum called "c" and sets its value to "Red".

How do you access and modify the values of enum instances in Solidity?
To access the value of an enum instance in Solidity, use the instance name. To modify the value of an enum instance, use the instance name followed by an assignment operator and one of the values in the enum.

Can you use enums as function parameters and mapping keys in Solidity?
Yes, in Solidity, enums can be passed as function parameters in the same way as other data types. Enums can also be used as keys in mappings, which are data structures that store key-value pairs. To use an enum as a mapping key, define the mapping using the enum name followed by the "=>" operator and the data type of the values. To access or modify a value in the mapping, use the mapping name followed by the key in square brackets.

INHERITANCE

In Solidity, inheritance is a mechanism that allows you to reuse code and extend the functionality of contracts by creating new contracts that are derived from existing ones. Inheritance is a key concept in programming that allows you to create more complex and powerful contracts by building upon the code and functionality of existing contracts. In this article, we'll take a closer look at inheritance in Solidity, including how to create derived contracts, how to access and override inherited functions, and how to use the "super" keyword to call inherited functions from derived contracts.

Defining Base Contracts

In Solidity, base contracts are contracts that are used as the foundation for derived contracts. Base contracts contain the code and functionality that will be inherited by the derived contracts.

To define a base contract, use the "contract" keyword followed by the contract name and a set of curly braces containing the contract's code and functionality. For example:

```
contract BaseContract {
  function baseFunction() public {
    console.log("This is a base function.");
  }
}
```

This code defines a base contract called "BaseContract" with a single function called "baseFunction" that prints a message to the console.

Creating Derived Contracts

To create a derived contract in Solidity, use the "contract" keyword followed by the contract name and the "is" keyword, and then the name of the base contract. The derived contract's code and functionality is defined within a set of curly braces as usual.

For example, the following code defines a derived contract called "DerivedContract" that is based on the "BaseContract" base contract:

```
contract DerivedContract is BaseContract {
  function derivedFunction() public {
    console.log("This is a derived function.");
  }
}
```

This code defines a derived contract called "DerivedContract" with a single function called "derivedFunction" that prints a message to the console. The "DerivedContract" contract also inherits the "baseFunction" function from the "BaseContract" base contract.

Accessing and Overriding Inherited Functions

In Solidity, derived contracts have access to all of the functions and variables of their base contracts. To access an inherited function, use the contract name followed by the function name.

For example:

```
DerivedContract d = new DerivedContract();
d.baseFunction();
```

This code creates a new instance of the "DerivedContract" contract called "d", and then calls the "baseFunction" function of the "BaseContract" base contract.

In some cases, you may want to override an inherited function in a derived contract. To override an inherited function, define a function with the same name and signature in the derived contract. The function in the derived contract will replace the inherited function and will be called instead of the inherited function when the function is called on an instance of the derived contract.

For example:

```
contract DerivedContract is BaseContract {
function baseFunction() public {
  console.log("This is an overridden function.");
}
}
```

This code defines a derived contract called "DerivedContract" that overrides the "baseFunction" function of the "BaseContract" base contract. When the "baseFunction" function is called on an instance of the "DerivedContract" contract, the overridden function will be called instead of the inherited function.

Using the "super" Keyword

In Solidity, the "super" keyword can be used to call an inherited function from within a derived contract. The "super" keyword is useful for calling inherited functions and then adding additional functionality to the derived contract.

For example:

```
contract DerivedContract is BaseContract {
function baseFunction() public {
  super.baseFunction();
  console.log("This is an extended function.");
```

```
}
```
```
}
```

This code defines a derived contract called "DerivedContract" that extends the "baseFunction" function of the "BaseContract" base contract. When the "baseFunction" function is called on an instance of the "DerivedContract" contract, the inherited "baseFunction" function will be called first using the "super" keyword, and then the additional functionality of the derived contract will be executed.

Conclusion

In conclusion, inheritance in Solidity is a powerful mechanism for reusing code and extending the functionality of contracts. Inheritance allows you to create more complex and powerful contracts by building upon the code and functionality of existing contracts, and it allows you to override inherited functions and extend them using the "super" keyword. Understanding inheritance is an important aspect of developing contracts and decentralized applications in Solidity.

Exercises

To review these concepts, we will go through a series of exercises designed to test your understanding and apply what you have learned.

What is inheritance in Solidity?
How do you create a base contract in Solidity?
How do you create a derived contract in Solidity?
How do you access and override inherited functions in Solidity?
How do you use the "super" keyword in Solidity?

Solutions

What is inheritance in Solidity?
In Solidity, inheritance is a mechanism that allows you to reuse code and extend the functionality of contracts by creating new contracts that are derived from existing ones. Inheritance is a key concept in programming that allows you to create more complex and powerful contracts by building upon the code and functionality of existing contracts.

How do you create a base contract in Solidity?
To create a base contract in Solidity, use the "contract" keyword followed by the contract name and a set of curly braces containing the contract's code and functionality. For example: "contract BaseContract { ... }". This code defines a base contract called "BaseContract" with the specified code and functionality.

How do you create a derived contract in Solidity?
To create a derived contract in Solidity, use the "contract" keyword followed by the contract name and the "is" keyword, and then the name of the base contract. The derived contract's code and functionality is defined within a set of curly braces as usual. For example: "contract DerivedContract is BaseContract { ... }". This code defines a derived contract called "DerivedContract" based on the "BaseContract" base contract.

How do you access and override inherited functions in Solidity?

In Solidity, derived contracts have access to all of the functions and variables of their base contracts. To access an inherited function, use the contract name followed by the function name. To override an inherited function, define a function with the same name and signature in the derived contract. The function in the derived contract will replace the inherited function and will be called instead of the inherited function when the function is called on an instance of the derived contract.

How do you use the "super" keyword in Solidity?

In Solidity, the "super" keyword can be used to call an inherited function from within a derived contract. The "super" keyword is useful for calling inherited functions and then adding additional functionality to the derived contract. To use the "super" keyword, call the inherited function using the "super" keyword followed by the function name. For example: "super.baseFunction();". This code calls the "baseFunction" function of the base contract from within a derived contract.

INTERFACES

In Solidity, interfaces are a mechanism that allow you to define a contract API (Application Programming Interface) and specify the functions and variables that a contract must implement. Interfaces are a key concept in programming that allow you to define a contract's API and ensure that it is implemented consistently across different contracts. In this article, we'll take a closer look at interfaces in Solidity, including how to define and use interfaces, how to implement interface functions in contracts, and how to interact with external contracts using interfaces.

Defining Interfaces

In Solidity, interfaces are defined using the "interface" keyword followed by the interface name and a set of curly braces containing the functions and variables that the interface defines. The functions and variables in an interface are called "interface functions" and "interface variables", respectively.

Interface functions and variables are defined in the same way as regular contract functions and variables, with the exception that they do not have a function body or variable value. Instead, they only specify the name, visibility, and parameter types of the functions and variables.

For example, the following code defines an interface called "SimpleInterface" with a single function called "function1":

```
interface SimpleInterface {
  function function1(uint256 a) public;
}
```

This code defines an interface called "SimpleInterface" with a single function called "function1" that takes a single "uint256" parameter called "a". The "public" visibility modifier specifies that the function can be called from any contract or external address.

Using Interfaces

In Solidity, interfaces are used to specify the functions and variables that a contract must implement. To use an interface in a contract, use the "is" keyword followed by the name of the interface.

For example:

```
contract SimpleContract is SimpleInterface {
  function function1(uint256 a) public {
    console.log("This is function1.");
```

```
}

}
```

This code defines a contract called "SimpleContract" that implements the "function1" function of the "SimpleInterface" interface. The "function1" function in the "SimpleContract" contract must have the same name, visibility, and parameter types as the "function1" function in the "SimpleInterface" interface.

Implementing Interface Functions

In Solidity, interface functions are implemented in contracts using the same syntax as regular contract functions. To implement an interface function, define a function with the same name, visibility, and parameter types as the interface function in the contract.

For example:

```
contract SimpleContract is SimpleInterface {
  function function1(uint256 a) public {
    console.log("This is function1.");
  }
}
```

This code defines a contract called "SimpleContract" that implements the "function1" function of the "SimpleInterface" interface. The "function1" function in the "SimpleContract" contract has the same name, visibility, and parameter types as the "function1" function in the "SimpleInterface" interface, and therefore satisfies the requirements of the interface.

Interacting with External Contracts

In Solidity, interfaces can be used to interact with external contracts in a type-safe manner. To interact with an external contract using an interface, use the "interface" keyword followed by the contract's address and the name of the interface.

For example:

```
contract SimpleContract {
  SimpleInterface externalContract = SimpleInterface(0x1234567890);
  function callExternalFunction() public {
    externalContract.function1(42);
  }
}
```

This code defines a contract called "SimpleContract" that interacts with an external contract at the address "0x1234567890" using the "SimpleInterface" interface. The "callExternalFunction" function in the "SimpleContract" contract calls the "function1" function of the external contract using the "externalContract" interface.

Interfaces and Type Checking

In Solidity, interfaces can be used to perform type checking on contracts and ensure that they implement the required functions and variables. To perform type checking on a contract using an interface, use the "is" keyword followed by the name of the interface and the contract instance.

For example:

```
contract SimpleContract {
function checkContractType(address contractAddress) public {
SimpleInterface contractInstance = SimpleInterface(contractAddress);
if (contractInstance.isSimpleInterface()) {
  console.log("This is a SimpleInterface contract.");
} else {
  console.log("This is not a SimpleInterface contract.");
 }
 }
}
```

This code defines a contract called "SimpleContract" that performs type checking on a contract instance using the "SimpleInterface" interface. The "checkContractType" function takes an "address" parameter called "contractAddress" and creates a contract instance using the "SimpleInterface" interface. The "isSimpleInterface" function is a built-in function in Solidity that returns "true" if the contract instance implements the "SimpleInterface" interface and "false" otherwise.

Conclusion

In conclusion, interfaces in Solidity are a powerful mechanism for defining contract APIs and interacting with external contracts. Interfaces allow you to specify the functions and variables that a contract must implement, and they enable you to perform type checking on contracts to ensure that they implement the required APIs. Understanding interfaces is an important aspect of developing contracts and decentralized applications in Solidity.

Exercises

To review these concepts, we will go through a series of exercises designed to test your understanding and apply what you have learned.

Implement an interface called Purchasable **that defines a function** buy() **which takes in an address of the buyer and returns a boolean indicating whether the purchase was successful.**
Create a contract called Product **that implements the** Purchasable**interface. The contract should have a public variable** price **of type** uint **and a constructor that sets the price of the product. The** buy()**function should check if the caller has sufficient balance to purchase the product and transfer the funds to the contract if the purchase is successful.**
Create a contract called Marketplace **that allows users to list** Purchasable **products for sale and**

purchase them. The contract should have a public mapping of products to their prices and a public function listProduct() that allows the caller to list a new product for sale. The buyProduct() function should take in the product's ID and the buyer's address and call the buy() function on the product contract.

In the Solidity contract below, create an interface called "Token" that has a function called "transfer" that takes in two arguments: a "to" address and an "amount" uint. The function should not have a return value.

```
pragma solidity ^0.7.0;
contract MyContract {
  // Your code here
}
```

In the Solidity contract below, create a struct called "User" that has two fields: a "name" string and an "age" uint. Then, create a mapping called "users" that maps a user's address to their User struct.

```
pragma solidity ^0.7.0;
contract MyContract {
  // Your code here
}
```

Solutions

Implement an interface called Purchasable that defines a function buy() which takes in an address of the buyer and returns a boolean indicating whether the purchase was successful.

```
pragma solidity ^0.7.0;
interface Purchasable {
  function buy(address buyer) external returns (bool);
}
```

Create a contract called Product that implements the Purchasable interface. The contract should have a public variable price of type uint and a constructor that sets the price of the product. The buy() function should check if the caller has sufficient balance to purchase the product and transfer the funds to the contract if the purchase is successful.

```
pragma solidity ^0.7.0;
import "https://github.com/OpenZeppelin/openzeppelin-solidity/contracts/math/SafeMath.sol";
interface Purchasable {
  function buy(address buyer) external returns (bool);
}
contract Product is Purchasable {
  using SafeMath for uint;
  uint public price;
```

```
constructor(uint _price) public {
  price = _price;
}
function buy(address buyer) public returns (bool) {
  require(buyer.balance >= price, "Insufficient balance");
  buyer.transfer(price);
  return true;
}
}
```

Create a contract called Marketplace **that allows users to list** Purchasable **products for sale and purchase them. The contract should have a public mapping of products to their prices and a public function** listProduct() **that allows the caller to list a new product for sale. The** buyProduct() **function should take in the product's ID and the buyer's address and call the** buy() **function on the product contract.**

```
pragma solidity ^0.7.0;
import "https://github.com/OpenZeppelin/openzeppelin-solidity/contracts/math/SafeMath.sol";
interface Purchasable {
  function buy(address buyer) external returns (bool);
}
contract Marketplace {
  mapping(uint => Purchasable) public products;
  mapping(uint => uint) public prices;
  function listProduct(Purchasable product, uint price) public {
    products[product.id()] = product;
    prices[product.id()] = price;
  }
  function buyProduct(uint productId, address buyer) public {
    require(products[productId].buy(buyer), "Purchase failed");
  }
}
```

In the Solidity contract below, create an interface called "Token" that has a function called "transfer" that takes in two arguments: a "to" address and an "amount" uint. The function should not have a return value.

```
pragma solidity ^0.7.0;
contract MyContract {
  // Your code here
```

```
}
```

Solution:

```
pragma solidity ^0.7.0;
contract MyContract {
  interface Token {
    function transfer(address to, uint amount) public;
  }
}
```

In the Solidity contract below, create a struct called "User" that has two fields: a "name" string and an "age" uint. Then, create a mapping called "users" that maps a user's address to their User struct.

```
pragma solidity ^0.7.0;
contract MyContract {
  // Your code here
}
```

Solution:

```
pragma solidity ^0.7.0;
contract MyContract {
  struct User {
    string name;
    uint age;
  }
  mapping(address => User) users;
}
```

WHAT IS A SMART CONTRACT?

Smart contracts are self-executing contracts with the terms of the agreement between buyer and seller being directly written into lines of code. The code and the agreements contained therein exist on the blockchain network. Smart contracts allow you to exchange money, property, shares, or anything of value in a transparent, conflict-free way while avoiding the services of a middleman. In this article, we'll take a closer look at the concept of smart contracts and how they work.

What is a Smart Contract?

A smart contract is a self-executing contract with the terms of the agreement between buyer and seller being directly written into lines of code. The code and the agreements contained therein exist on the blockchain network.

Smart contracts were first proposed by Nick Szabo, a computer scientist, in 1994. Szabo defined a smart contract as "a computerized transaction protocol that executes the terms of a contract." He saw the potential for using smart contracts to facilitate, verify, and enforce the negotiation or performance of a contract.

How Do Smart Contracts Work?

Smart contracts work by using blockchain technology to create a secure, transparent, and tamper-proof record of the agreement. A smart contract consists of a set of rules and conditions that are encoded into the blockchain network. When the conditions of the contract are met, the terms of the agreement are automatically executed.

For example, consider a smart contract that automates the process of buying and selling a house. The contract might contain conditions such as the price of the house, the closing date, and the ownership transfer. When the buyer and seller agree to the terms of the contract and execute the transaction, the contract is recorded on the blockchain network. When the closing date arrives and the buyer pays the agreed-upon price, the ownership of the house is automatically transferred to the buyer.

Benefits of Smart Contracts

There are several benefits to using smart contracts:

- Smart contracts are transparent: The terms of the agreement are encoded in the contract and recorded on the blockchain network, making them transparent and easy to verify.
- Smart contracts are secure: The blockchain network is highly secure, making it difficult for hackers to tamper with the contract.
- Smart contracts are faster: Because the terms of the agreement are automatically executed, the process is faster and more efficient than traditional contract negotiation

and execution.

- Smart contracts reduce the need for intermediaries: Because the contract is self-executing, the need for intermediaries such as lawyers or brokers is reduced. This can save time and money.
- Smart contracts are immutable: Once the contract is recorded on the blockchain network, it cannot be altered. This ensures that the terms of the agreement are maintained and cannot be changed.

Applications of Smart Contracts

Smart contracts have the potential to revolutionize a wide range of industries and applications. Some examples of industries that could benefit from smart contracts include:

- Real estate: Smart contracts could streamline the process of buying and selling property by automating the transfer of ownership and reducing the need for intermediaries.
- Supply chain management: Smart contracts could be used to track the movement of goods and ensure that all parties in the supply chain are paid on time.
- Insurance: Smart contracts could automate the claims process and reduce the need for manual claims processing.
- Government: Smart contracts could be used to automate government services such as the issuance of licenses and permits.
- Banking and finance: Smart contracts could be used to automate financial transactions such as the execution of trades and the clearing and settlement of securities.

Conclusion

Smart contracts are self-executing contracts with the terms of the agreement between buyer and seller being directly written into lines of code. Smart contracts allow you to exchange money, property, shares, or anything of value in a transparent, conflict-free way while avoiding the services of a middleman. Smart contracts have the potential to revolutionize a wide range of industries and applications, including real estate, supply chain management, insurance, government, and banking and finance.

Exercises

To review these concepts, we will go through a series of exercises designed to test your understanding and apply what you have learned.

What is a smart contract?
How do smart contracts work?
What are the benefits of using smart contracts?
What are some examples of industries that could benefit from smart contracts?
How do smart contracts reduce the need for intermediaries?

Solutions

What is a smart contract?
A smart contract is a self-executing contract with the terms of the agreement between buyer and seller being directly written into lines of code. The code and the agreements contained therein exist on the blockchain network.

How do smart contracts work?
Smart contracts work by using blockchain technology to create a secure, transparent, and tamper-proof record of the agreement. A smart contract consists of a set of rules and conditions that are encoded into the blockchain network. When the conditions of the contract are met, the terms of the agreement are automatically executed.

What are the benefits of using smart contracts?
Some benefits of using smart contracts include transparency, security, speed, reduced need for intermediaries, and immutability.

What are some examples of industries that could benefit from smart contracts?
Some examples of industries that could benefit from smart contracts include real estate, supply chain management, insurance, government, and banking and finance.

How do smart contracts reduce the need for intermediaries?
Smart contracts reduce the need for intermediaries such as lawyers or brokers because the contract is self-executing. This can save time and money.

EXAMPLES OF SMART CONTRACTS

Smart contracts are self-executing contracts with the terms of the agreement between buyer and seller being directly written into lines of code. The code and the agreements contained therein exist on the blockchain network. Smart contracts have the potential to revolutionize a wide range of industries and applications, including real estate, supply chain management, insurance, government, and banking and finance. In this article, we'll take a closer look at some examples of smart contracts in action.

Real Estate

One potential application of smart contracts is in the real estate industry. Smart contracts could streamline the process of buying and selling property by automating the transfer of ownership and reducing the need for intermediaries.

For example, consider a smart contract that automates the process of buying and selling a house. The contract might contain conditions such as the price of the house, the closing date, and the ownership transfer. When the buyer and seller agree to the terms of the contract and execute the transaction, the contract is recorded on the blockchain network. When the closing date arrives and the buyer pays the agreed-upon price, the ownership of the house is automatically transferred to the buyer.

Supply Chain Management

Another potential application of smart contracts is in supply chain management. Smart contracts could be used to track the movement of goods and ensure that all parties in the supply chain are paid on time.

For example, consider a smart contract that is used to track the movement of a shipment of goods from the manufacturer to the retailer. The contract might contain conditions such as the price of the goods, the delivery date, and the payment terms. As the goods move through the supply chain, the contract is updated with the relevant information. When the goods are delivered to the retailer, the payment is automatically released to the manufacturer.

Insurance

Smart contracts could also be used to automate the claims process in the insurance industry. By using smart contracts, insurers could streamline the claims process and reduce the need for manual claims processing.

For example, consider a smart contract that is used to process a car insurance claim. The contract might contain conditions such as the policy holder's coverage limits, the details of the accident, and the estimates for repair costs. When the policy holder submits a claim, the contract is automatically updated with the relevant information. If the claim meets the terms of the policy, the payment is automatically released to the policy holder.

Government

Smart contracts could be used to automate government services such as the issuance of licenses and permits. By using smart contracts, governments could streamline the process of providing services and reduce the need for manual processing.

For example, consider a smart contract that is used to issue a driver's license. The contract might contain conditions such as the applicant's personal information, driving history, and test results. When the applicant applies for a license, the contract is automatically updated with the relevant information. If the applicant meets the requirements for a license, the license is automatically issued.

Banking and Finance

Smart contracts could also be used to automate financial transactions such as the execution of trades and the clearing and settlement of securities. By using smart contracts, banks and financial institutions could streamline the process of processing transactions and reduce the need for manual processing.

For example, consider a smart contract that is used to execute a stock trade. The contract might contain conditions such as the price of the stock, the number of shares, and the settlement date. When the trade is executed, the contract is automatically updated with the relevant information. When the settlement date arrives, the payment is automatically released to the seller and the shares are transferred to the buyer.

Conclusion

Smart contracts are self-executing contracts with the terms of the agreement between buyer and seller being directly written into lines of code. Smart contracts have the potential to revolutionize a wide range of industries and applications, including real estate, supply chain management, insurance, government, and banking and finance.

In the real estate industry, smart contracts could streamline the process of buying and selling property by automating the transfer of ownership and reducing the need for intermediaries. In supply chain management, smart contracts could be used to track the movement of goods and ensure that all parties in the supply chain are paid on time. In the insurance industry, smart contracts could automate the claims process and reduce the need for manual claims processing. In government, smart contracts could be used to automate the issuance of licenses and permits. And in banking and finance, smart contracts could be used to automate financial transactions such as the execution of trades and the clearing and settlement of securities.

Smart contracts have the potential to transform the way we do business and interact with each other. As the use of blockchain technology continues to grow, we can expect to see more and more real-world applications of smart contracts in the future.

Exercises

To review these concepts, we will go through a series of exercises designed to test your understanding and apply what you have learned.

What is a smart contract?
How could smart contracts be used in the real estate industry?
How could smart contracts be used in supply chain management?
How could smart contracts be used in the insurance industry?
How could smart contracts be used in banking and finance?

Solutions

What is a smart contract?
A smart contract is a self-executing contract with the terms of the agreement between buyer and seller being directly written into lines of code. The code and the agreements contained therein exist on the blockchain network.

How could smart contracts be used in the real estate industry?
Smart contracts could be used in the real estate industry to streamline the process of buying and selling property by automating the transfer of ownership and reducing the need for intermediaries.

How could smart contracts be used in supply chain management?
Smart contracts could be used in supply chain management to track the movement of goods and ensure that all parties in the supply chain are paid on time.

How could smart contracts be used in the insurance industry?
Smart contracts could be used in the insurance industry to automate the claims process and reduce the need for manual claims processing.

How could smart contracts be used in banking and finance?
Smart contracts could be used in banking and finance to automate financial transactions such as the execution of trades and the clearing and settlement of securities.

WRITING A SIMPLE SMART CONTRACT

Smart contracts are self-executing contracts with the terms of the agreement between buyer and seller being directly written into lines of code. Smart contracts have the potential to revolutionize a wide range of industries and applications, including real estate, supply chain management, insurance, government, and banking and finance. In this article, we'll take a look at the basics of writing a simple smart contract using Solidity, a programming language specifically designed for writing smart contracts on the Ethereum blockchain.

Getting Started

Before you can write a smart contract, you'll need to set up a development environment. There are several options available, but one of the most popular is Truffle, a development framework for Ethereum. To install Truffle, you'll need to have Node.js and npm (the Node Package Manager) installed on your computer.

Once you've installed Node.js and npm, you can install Truffle by running the following command:

```
npm install -g truffle
```

With Truffle installed, you're ready to create a new project. To do so, open a terminal and navigate to the directory where you want to create your project. Then run the following command:

```
truffle init
```

This will create a new project directory with the following structure:

```
my-project/
├── contracts/
│   └── Migrations.sol
├── migrations/
│   └── 1_initial_migration.js
├── test/
├── truffle-config.js
└── truffle.js
```

The contracts directory is where you'll write your smart contracts. The migrations directory is where you'll write scripts to deploy your smart contracts to the blockchain. The test directory is where you'll write tests for your smart contracts. And the truffle-config.js and truffle.js files are configuration files for Truffle.

Writing Your First Smart Contract

Now that you have a project set up, you're ready to write your first smart contract. To do so, create a new file in the contracts directory called MyContract.sol. This is where you'll write your contract code.

The first thing you'll need to do is specify the contract's version and import any necessary libraries. You can do this at the top of your contract file like this:

```solidity
pragma solidity ^0.5.11;
import "https://github.com/OpenZeppelin/openzeppelin-solidity/contracts/math/SafeMath.sol";
```

The pragma solidity line specifies the version of Solidity that you're using. The import line imports the SafeMath library from OpenZeppelin, which provides functions for safe arithmetic operations.

Next, you'll need to define your contract. You can do this by writing a contract block like this:

```solidity
contract MyContract {

}
```

Inside the contract block, you can define variables, functions, and other elements of your contract. For example, you might define a variable like this:

```solidity
contract MyContract {
  uint public myVariable;

}
```

This defines a public variable called myVariable that is of type uint (unsigned integer). The public keyword makes the variable accessible from outside the contract.

You can also define functions in your contract. For example, you might define a function like this:

```solidity
contract MyContract {
  function myFunction() public {
    // function code goes here
  }

}
```

This defines a public function called myFunction. The public keyword makes the function accessible from outside the contract.

You can also specify the visibility and mutability of your functions and variables. The visibility of a function or variable determines who can access it, while the mutability determines whether it can be modified. There are four visibility levels in Solidity: public, internal, external, and private. There are two mutability levels: pure and view.

The public visibility level makes the function or variable accessible from outside the contract. The internal visibility level makes the function or variable accessible only within the contract and any contracts that inherit from it. The external visibility level makes the function accessible only from outside the contract, but not from within it. And the private visibility level makes the function or variable accessible only within the contract.

The pure mutability level indicates that the function does not modify the state of the contract and does not depend on any state variables. The view mutability level indicates that the function does not modify the state of the contract, but may depend on state variables.

Here's an example of a function with both visibility and mutability levels specified:

```
contract MyContract {
  function myFunction() external pure {
    // function code goes here
  }
}
```

This function is called myFunction and it is both external (meaning it can be called from outside the contract) and pure (meaning it does not modify the state of the contract and does not depend on any state variables).

Deploying Your Smart Contract

Once you've written your smart contract, you'll need to deploy it to the blockchain. To do so, you'll need to create a migration script in the migrations directory.

A migration script is a JavaScript file that contains instructions for deploying your smart contract to the blockchain. To create a new migration script, create a new file in the migrations directory with a filename that begins with a number, followed by an underscore and a description of the migration. For example, you might create a file called 2_deploy_my_contract.js.

In your migration script, you'll need to specify the contract that you want to deploy and any arguments that you want to pass to the contract's constructor. The constructor is a special function that is executed when the contract is deployed. It is used to initialize the contract's state.

Here's an example of a migration script that deploys the MyContract contract:

```
const MyContract = artifacts.require("MyContract");
module.exports = function(deployer) {
  deployer.deploy(MyContract);
};
```

This script uses the artifacts.require function to require the compiled version of the MyContract contract. It then exports a function that takes a deployer as an argument. The deployer is an object that provides methods for deploying contracts.

In this example, the deployer.deploy method is used to deploy the MyContract contract. This method takes the contract as an argument and returns a promise that is resolved when the contract is deployed.

To deploy your contract, run the following command in your terminal:

```
truffle migrate
```

This will run your migration scripts and deploy your contracts to the blockchain.

Testing Your Smart Contract

Once you've deployed your smart contract, you'll want to test it to make sure it's working as expected. To do so, you can write tests using the Truffle testing framework.

To create a test, create a new file in the test directory with a filename that ends in .test.js. For example, you might create a file called my_contract.test.js.

In your test file, you'll need to require the compiled version of your contract and any libraries that you want to use. You can do this at the top of your file like this:

```
const MyContract = artifacts.require("MyContract");
const truffleAssert = require("truffle-assertions");
```

The artifacts.require function is used to require the compiled version of the MyContract contract. The truffleAssert library is a collection of assertion functions that make it easier to write tests.

Next, you'll need to write a test function. A test function is a function that contains one or more test cases. To write a test function, use the test keyword followed by a description of the test case. For example:

```
test("My test case", async () => {
    // test code goes here
});
```

Inside the test function, you can use the truffleAssert library to make assertions about the state of your contract. For example, you might assert that a function returns the expected value like this:

```
truffleAssert.equal(actualValue, expectedValue, "Values should be equal");
```

You can also use the truffleAssert library to assert that a transaction was successful or that an event was emitted.

To run your tests, run the following command in your terminal:

```
truffle test
```

This will run all the test files in your test directory and report the results.

Conclusion

In this article, we've covered the basics of writing a simple smart contract using Solidity. We've looked at how to set up a development environment, how to define variables and functions in a contract, how to deploy the contract to the blockchain, and how to write tests for the contract.

There is much more to learn about Solidity and smart contracts, including advanced concepts like contract inheritance, contract interfaces, and security considerations. With the knowledge you've gained from this article, you can continue learning and experimenting with Solidity and the Ethereum blockchain to build more complex and powerful contracts.

Exercises

To review these concepts, we will go through a series of exercises designed to test your understanding and apply what you have learned.

Write a smart contract that defines a variable called "name" and a function called "setName" that sets the value of the name variable. Deploy the contract and test that the setName function works as expected.

Write a smart contract that defines a function called "add" that takes two arguments and returns their sum. Deploy the contract and test that the add function works as expected.

Write a smart contract that defines a struct called "Person" with fields for a name and an age. Write a function called "createPerson" that takes a name and an age as arguments and returns a Person struct. Deploy the contract and test that the createPerson function works as expected.

Write a smart contract that defines a mapping called "ages" that maps addresses to ages. Write a function called "setAge" that takes an address and an age as arguments and sets the age for the given address in the mapping. Write a function called "getAge" that takes an address as an argument and returns the age for the given address from the mapping. Deploy the contract and test that the setAge and getAge functions work as expected.

Write a smart contract that defines an enum called "Color" with values "Red", "Green", and "Blue". Write a function called "setColor" that takes a Color as an argument and sets a variable called "favoriteColor" to the given Color. Write a function called "getColor" that returns the value of the favoriteColor variable. Deploy the contract and test that the setColor and getColor functions work as expected.

Exercises

Write a smart contract that defines a variable called "name" and a function called "setName" that sets the value of the name variable. Deploy the contract and test that the setName function works as expected.

```solidity
pragma solidity ^0.8.0;
contract NameContract {
string name;
function setName(string memory _name) public {
  name = _name;
}
}
```

To test this contract, you can use the following test code:

```
const NameContract = artifacts.require("NameContract");
const truffleAssert = require("truffle-assertions");
contract("NameContract", () => {
 it("should set the name correctly", async () => {
  const contract = await NameContract.deployed();
  await contract.setName("Alice");
  const result = await contract.name();
  assert.equal(result, "Alice", "Name was not set correctly");
 });
});
```

Write a smart contract that defines a function called "add" that takes two arguments and returns their sum. Deploy the contract and test that the add function works as expected.

```
pragma solidity ^0.8.0;
contract AddContract {
 function add(uint a, uint b) public pure returns (uint) {
  return a + b;
 }
}
```

To test this contract, you can use the following test code:

```
const AddContract = artifacts.require("AddContract");
const truffleAssert = require("truffle-assertions");
contract("AddContract", () => {
 it("should add two numbers correctly", async () => {
  const contract = await AddContract.deployed();
  const result = await contract.add(2, 3);
  assert.equal(result, 5, "Numbers were not added correctly");
 });
});
```

Write a smart contract that defines a struct called "Person" with fields for a name and an age. Write a function called "createPerson" that takes a name and an age as arguments and returns a Person struct. Deploy the contract and test that the createPerson function works as expected.

```
pragma solidity ^0.8.0;
contract PersonContract {
 struct Person {
```

```solidity
  string name;
  uint age;
}
function createPerson(string memory _name, uint _age) public pure returns (Person memory) {
  Person memory person;
  person.name = _name;
  person.age = _age;
  return person;
}
}
```

To test this contract, you can use the following test code:

```javascript
const PersonContract = artifacts.require("PersonContract");
const truffleAssert = require("truffle-assertions");
contract("PersonContract", () => {
 it("should create a person correctly", async () => {
  const contract = await PersonContract.deployed();
  const result = await contract.createPerson("Alice", 30);
  assert.equal(result.name, "Alice", "Name was not set correctly");
  assert.equal(result.age, 30, "Age was not set correctly");
 });
});
```

Write a smart contract that defines a mapping called "ages" that maps addresses to ages. Write a function called "setAge" that takes an address and an age as arguments and sets the age for the given address in the mapping. Write a function called "getAge" that takes an address as an argument and returns the age for the given address from the mapping. Deploy the contract and test that the setAge and getAge functions work as expected.

```solidity
pragma solidity ^0.8.0;
contract AgeContract {
 mapping(address => uint) public ages;
 function setAge(address _address, uint _age) public {
  ages[_address] = _age;
 }
 function getAge(address _address) public view returns (uint) {
  return ages[_address];
 }
}
```

To test this contract, you can use the following test code:

```
const AgeContract = artifacts.require("AgeContract");
const truffleAssert = require("truffle-assertions");
contract("AgeContract", () => {
 it("should set and get an age correctly", async () => {
  const contract = await AgeContract.deployed();
  await contract.setAge(accounts[0], 30);
  const result = await contract.getAge(accounts[0]);
  assert.equal(result, 30, "Age was not set or retrieved correctly");
 });
});
```

Write a smart contract that defines an enum called "Color" with values "Red", "Green", and "Blue". Write a function called "setColor" that takes a Color as an argument and sets a variable called "favoriteColor" to the given Color. Write a function called "getColor" that returns the value of the favoriteColor variable. Deploy the contract and test that the setColor and getColor functions work as expected.

```
pragma solidity ^0.8.0;
contract ColorContract {
 enum Color { Red, Green, Blue }
 Color public favoriteColor;
 function setColor(Color _color) public {
  favoriteColor = _color;
 }
 function getColor() public view returns (Color) {
  return favoriteColor;
 }
}
```

To test this contract, you can use the following test code:

```
const ColorContract = artifacts.require("ColorContract");
const truffleAssert = require("truffle-assertions");
contract("ColorContract", () => {
 it("should set and get a color correctly", async () => {
  const contract = await ColorContract.deployed();
  await contract.setColor(1);
  const result = await contract.getColor();
  assert.equal(result, 1, "Color was not set or retrieved correctly");
```

```
});
});
```

DEPLOYING SMART CONTRACTS ON THE ETHEREUM NETWORK

In this article, we will explore the process of deploying smart contracts on the Ethereum network. As we learned in previous articles, a smart contract is a program that is stored on the Ethereum blockchain and can be executed by anyone. In order to make a smart contract available for others to use, it must be deployed to the Ethereum network.

Prerequisites

Before we can deploy a smart contract to the Ethereum network, we need to set up a few things:

- A development environment for writing and testing Solidity code. We covered this in the "Setting up a development environment" article.
- A local Ethereum blockchain for testing. We can use tools like Ganache or Truffle Develop for this.
- An Ethereum wallet for signing transactions. We can use tools like MetaMask or MyEthereumWallet for this.

Deploying a Smart Contract

There are a few steps involved in deploying a smart contract to the Ethereum network:

1. Write the Solidity code for the contract.
2. Compile the contract to generate the bytecode and ABI (Application Binary Interface).
3. Deploy the contract to the Ethereum network using a transaction.
4. Interact with the contract using its ABI.

Let's go through each of these steps in more detail.

Writing the Solidity Code

First, we need to write the Solidity code for our smart contract. This can be done using any text editor or code editor that supports Solidity. Here is an example of a simple contract that stores a message:

```solidity
pragma solidity ^0.8.0;
contract MessageContract {
 string public message;
 constructor(string memory _message) public {
  message = _message;
 }
}
```

```
}
```

This contract has a single public variable called "message" of type string, and a constructor function that sets the value of the message variable when the contract is deployed.

Compiling the Contract

Once we have written the Solidity code for our contract, we need to compile it to generate the bytecode and ABI. The bytecode is the code that is actually stored on the Ethereum blockchain and executed by the Ethereum Virtual Machine (EVM). The ABI is a JSON representation of the contract's functions and their inputs and outputs, which allows us to interact with the contract using web3.js or other Ethereum libraries.

We can use a tool like Remix or Truffle to compile our contract. For example, using Remix, we can paste our Solidity code into the left panel and click the "Compile" button to see the compiled bytecode and ABI in the right panel.

Deploying the Contract

Once we have the compiled bytecode and ABI, we are ready to deploy the contract to the Ethereum network. This is done using a transaction that creates a new contract on the blockchain. To create the transaction, we need to do the following:

1. Load the compiled bytecode and ABI into our Ethereum wallet or client.
2. Sign the transaction using our private key.
3. Send the signed transaction to the Ethereum network.

The exact process will depend on the Ethereum wallet or client we are using. For example, using MetaMask, we can click the "Deploy Contract" button, enter the bytecode and ABI, and click "Submit" to send the transaction.

Interacting with the Contract

Once the contract has been deployed, we can interact with it using its ABI. The ABI allows us to call functions on the contract and read or write data from its variables. For example, using web3.js, we can use the ABI to create a contract object and call its functions like this:

```
const contract = new web3.eth.Contract(abi, contractAddress);
contract.methods.message().call().then(console.log);
```

This code creates a contract object using the ABI and the contract's address on the Ethereum network, and then calls the "message" function to retrieve the value of the "message" variable.

Conclusion

In this article, we learned about the process of deploying smart contracts to the Ethereum network. We covered the steps of writing the Solidity code, compiling the contract, deploying it using a transaction, and interacting with the contract using its ABI. Deploying smart contracts is an important step in making them available for others to use, and understanding the process is crucial for building decentralized applications on Ethereum.

Exercises

To review these concepts, we will go through a series of exercises designed to test your understanding and apply what you have learned.

Deploy the MessageContract contract from the example above to your local Ethereum network using Ganache or Truffle Develop.

Interact with the contract using its ABI and web3.js. Try calling the "message" function and changing the value of the "message" variable.

Write a contract that stores a simple voting system. The contract should have a function for adding candidates and a function for voting for a candidate.

Deploy the voting contract to your local Ethereum network and test it using web3.js.

Modify the voting contract to store votes on the blockchain using the "mapping" data structure. Test the modified contract to make sure it is working correctly.

Deploy the MessageContract contract from the example above to your local Ethereum network using Ganache or Truffle Develop.

1. To deploy the MessageContract contract using Ganache or Truffle Develop, you will need to follow these steps:
   - Compile the contract using Remix or Truffle.
   - Load the compiled bytecode and ABI into your Ethereum wallet or client.
   - Sign the transaction using your private key.
   - Send the signed transaction to the Ethereum network using Ganache or Truffle Develop.

Interact with the contract using its ABI and web3.js. Try calling the "message" function and changing the value of the "message" variable.

To interact with the contract using its ABI and web3.js, you can use the following code:

```
const contract = new web3.eth.Contract(abi, contractAddress);
// Call the "message" function to retrieve the value of the "message" variable
contract.methods.message().call().then(console.log);
// Change the value of the "message" variable by calling the "setMessage" function
contract.methods.setMessage("Hello, world!").send({ from: accounts[0] });
```

Write a contract that stores a simple voting system. The contract should have a function for adding candidates and a function for voting for a candidate.

3. Here is an example of a contract that stores a simple voting system:

```
pragma solidity ^0.8.0;
contract VotingContract {
 struct Candidate {
  string name;
  uint votes;
 }
 mapping(uint => Candidate) public candidates;
```

```solidity
uint public numCandidates;
function addCandidate(string memory _name) public {
candidates[numCandidates] = Candidate(_name, 0);
numCandidates++;
}
function vote(uint _candidateIndex) public {
candidates[_candidateIndex].votes++;
}
}
```

Deploy the voting contract to your local Ethereum network and test it using web3.js.

4. To deploy the voting contract to your local Ethereum network and test it using web3.js, you can follow these steps:
   - Compile the contract using Remix or Truffle.
   - Load the compiled bytecode and ABI into your Ethereum wallet or client.
   - Sign the transaction using your private key.
   - Send the signed transaction to the Ethereum network using Ganache or Truffle Develop.
   - Use web3.js to create a contract object and call its functions.

For example:

```javascript
const contract = new web3.eth.Contract(abi, contractAddress);
// Add a candidate
contract.methods.addCandidate("Alice").send({ from: accounts[0] });
// Vote for a candidate
contract.methods.vote(0).send({ from: accounts[0] });
```

Modify the voting contract to store votes on the blockchain using the "mapping" data structure. Test the modified contract to make sure it is working correctly.

To modify the voting contract to store votes on the blockchain using the "mapping" data structure, you can use the following code:

```solidity
pragma solidity ^0.8.0;
contract VotingContract {
struct Candidate {
string name;
uint votes;
}
mapping(address => bool) public voted;
mapping(uint => Candidate) public candidates;
uint public numCandidates;
```

```solidity
function addCandidate(string memory _name) public {
    candidates[numCandidates] = Candidate(_name, 0);
    numCandidates++;
}

function vote(uint _candidateIndex) public {
    require(!voted[msg.sender], "You have already voted.");
    voted[msg.sender] = true;
    candidates[_candidateIndex].votes++;
}
}
```

This code adds a "voted" mapping that stores a boolean value for each address, indicating whether the address has already voted. The "vote" function checks this value before incrementing the candidate's vote count, to ensure that each address can only vote once.

INTERACTING WITH SMART CONTRACTS USING WEB3.JS

To use web3.js, you will need to include the library in your project. You can either download the library from the web3.js GitHub repository and include it in your project manually, or you can use a package manager like npm to install it.

Once you have web3.js installed, you can create a web3 instance by connecting to an Ethereum node. An Ethereum node is a server that maintains a copy of the Ethereum blockchain and allows you to send transactions and read data from the blockchain. You can use a public Ethereum node, like Infura, or you can run your own node using software like Geth or Parity.

To create a web3 instance, you will need to provide the URL of the Ethereum node and the ABI of the smart contract you want to interact with. The ABI is a JSON object that defines the functions and variables of the contract, and is generated when the contract is compiled. Here is an example of how to create a web3 instance using Infura and a contract ABI:

```
const Web3 = require('web3');
const web3 = new Web3('https://mainnet.infura.io/v3/YOUR-API-KEY');
const contractABI = require('./contractABI.json');
// Create a contract object using the ABI
const contract = new web3.eth.Contract(contractABI, contractAddress);
```

Reading and Writing Data

Once you have a web3 instance and a contract object, you can call functions on the contract and read or write data from its variables. To call a function, you can use the "methods" property of the contract object and pass the function name and any arguments. For example, to call a function named "getMessage" that returns a string, you can use the following code:

```
contract.methods.getMessage().call().then((result) => {
  console.log(result);
});
```

To write data to a contract, you will need to create and sign a transaction using the "send" method of the contract object. The "send" method takes an object with the transaction details, such as the gas limit and the value to be transferred. Here is an example of how to call a function named "setMessage" that sets a string variable:

```
contract.methods.setMessage("Hello, world!").send({
  from: accounts[0],
  gas: 1000000,
  value: 0
});
```

Listening for Events

Smart contracts can emit events when certain conditions are met. For example, a contract might emit an event when a new user is registered or when a payment is made. You can use web3.js to listen for these events and take action when they are emitted.

To listen for events, you can use the "events" property of the contract object and pass the event name and any filters. For example, to listen for a "NewMessage" event that has a string argument, you can use the following code:

```
contract.events.NewMessage({}, (error, event) => {
  if (error) {
    console.error(error);
  } else {
    console.log(event.returnValues.message);
  }
});
```

This code will log the value of the "message" argument every time the "NewMessage" event is emitted. You can also use filters to narrow down the events you want to listen to. For example, you can specify a block range or a specific address to listen for events from.

```
contract.events.NewMessage({
  fromBlock: 0,
  toBlock: 'latest'
}, (error, event) => {
  if (error) {
    console.error(error);
  } else {
    console.log(event.returnValues.message);
  }
});
```

This code will listen for events from all blocks in the Ethereum blockchain. You can also specify a block range or a specific address to listen for events from.

Best Practices

Here are some best practices for using web3.js in a production environment:

- Use a public Ethereum node like Infura for production, as it is more reliable and secure than running your own node.
- Use a library like Web3-Utils to handle common tasks like formatting and validating Ethereum addresses and transaction hashes.
- Use a library like Async-Web3 to handle asynchronous tasks like waiting for transactions to be mined.
- Use a library like Web3-Provider-Engine to cache and retry failed requests, and to add middleware like rate limiting and transaction signing.
- Use a library like Web3-Ethers to sign transactions using private keys stored in a secure environment like a hardware wallet.

Conclusion

In this article, we learned how to use web3.js to interact with smart contracts on the Ethereum blockchain. We saw how to read and write data from contracts, and how to listen for events emitted by the contracts. We also looked at some best practices for using web3.js in a production environment. By using web3.js, you can build decentralized applications that leverage the power of the Ethereum network and smart contracts.

Exercises

To review these concepts, we will go through a series of exercises designed to test your understanding and apply what you have learned.

Write a function that takes a contract object and a message string as arguments, and calls the "setMessage" function on the contract with the message as the argument. The function should return the transaction receipt.

Write a function that takes a contract object as an argument and calls the "getMessage" function on the contract. The function should return the value of the message string.

Write a function that takes a contract object as an argument and listens for "NewMessage" events. The function should log the value of the message string every time the event is emitted.

Write a function that takes a contract object and a block number as arguments and listens for "NewMessage" events from the specified block. The function should log the value of the message string every time the event is emitted.

Write a function that takes a contract object, a block number, and an address as arguments and listens for "NewMessage" events from the specified block and address. The function should log the value of the message string every time the event is emitted.

Solutions

Write a function that takes a contract object and a message string as arguments, and calls the "setMessage" function on the contract with the message as the argument. The function should return the transaction receipt.

```
function setMessage(contract, message) {
```

```
return contract.methods.setMessage(message).send({
  from: accounts[0],
  gas: 1000000,
  value: 0
}).then((receipt) => {
  return receipt;
});
}
```

Write a function that takes a contract object as an argument and calls the "getMessage" function on the contract. The function should return the value of the message string.

```
function getMessage(contract) {
  return contract.methods.getMessage().call().then((result) => {
    return result;
  });
}
```

Write a function that takes a contract object as an argument and listens for "NewMessage" events. The function should log the value of the message string every time the event is emitted.

```
function listenForNewMessage(contract) {
  contract.events.NewMessage({}, (error, event) => {
    if (error) {
      console.error(error);
    } else {
      console.log(event.returnValues.message);
    }
  });
}
```

Write a function that takes a contract object and a block number as arguments and listens for "NewMessage" events from the specified block. The function should log the value of the message string every time the event is emitted.

```
function listenForNewMessageFromBlock(contract, blockNumber) {
  contract.events.NewMessage({
    fromBlock: blockNumber
  }, (error, event) => {
    if (error) {
      console.error(error);
```

```
  } else {
    console.log(event.returnValues.message);
  }
});
}
```

Write a function that takes a contract object, a block number, and an address as arguments and listens for "NewMessage" events from the specified block and address. The function should log the value of the message string every time the event is emitted.

```
function listenForNewMessageFromBlockAndAddress(contract, blockNumber, address) {
contract.events.NewMessage({
  fromBlock: blockNumber,
  filter: {
    _from: address
  }
}, (error, event) => {
  if (error) {
    console.error(error);
  } else {
    console.log(event.returnValues.message);
  }
});
}
```

COMMON VULNERABILITIES IN SOLIDITY

As a programming language, Solidity is susceptible to vulnerabilities just like any other language. It is important for developers to be aware of these vulnerabilities and take steps to avoid them when writing smart contracts. In this article, we will discuss some common vulnerabilities in Solidity and how to avoid them.

Reentrancy

Reentrancy is a vulnerability that occurs when a contract calls another contract and that contract is able to call back into the original contract before the original contract has finished executing. This can lead to an infinite loop and result in the contract running out of gas.

To avoid reentrancy vulnerabilities, it is important to follow these best practices:

- Use the "lock" pattern to prevent reentrancy by setting a flag when a contract function is executing, and checking the flag before executing any functions that could potentially call back into the contract.
- Use the "check-effects-interactions" pattern to prevent reentrancy by separating the functions that check conditions from the functions that execute actions. This ensures that the contract can complete all its checks before executing any actions.

Unchecked Send

The Solidity "send" function is used to transfer value from a contract to another contract or external address. However, the "send" function does not return a value, so it is possible for the "send" function to fail without the contract being aware of it. This can lead to the contract being in an unexpected state and potentially vulnerable to attack.

To avoid unchecked send vulnerabilities, it is important to follow these best practices:

- Use the "require" function to check the return value of the "send" function and ensure that it was successful.
- Use the "transfer" function instead of "send" whenever possible, as "transfer" will throw an exception if it fails, which allows the contract to catch the exception and take appropriate action.

Uninitialized Storage Pointers

In Solidity, it is possible to declare storage pointers that are not initialized with a value. If these pointers are not initialized, they will point to an arbitrary location in storage and could potentially overwrite important data.

To avoid uninitialized storage pointers, it is important to follow these best practices:

- Always initialize storage pointers with a value before using them.
- Use the "memory" keyword to declare variables that are stored in memory and not in storage.

Integer Overflow/Underflow

In Solidity, integers are not checked for overflow or underflow, which means that it is possible for an integer to exceed its maximum or minimum value and wrap around. This can lead to unexpected results and potentially vulnerable code.

To avoid integer overflow/underflow vulnerabilities, it is important to follow these best practices:

- Use the "SafeMath" library to handle arithmetic operations, as it includes functions that check for overflow/underflow and throw an exception if it occurs.
- Use the "require" function to check that integers are within the expected range before performing any operations on them.

Race Conditions

Race conditions occur when two or more transactions are trying to update the same data at the same time, and the final result depends on the order in which the transactions are processed. This can lead to unexpected results and potentially vulnerable code.

To avoid race conditions, it is important to follow these best practices:

- Use the "mutex" pattern to prevent race conditions by setting a flag when a contract function is executing, and checking the flag before executing any functions that could potentially update the same data.
- Use the "atomic" pattern to prevent race conditions by grouping multiple transactions into a single atomic transaction that either executes all the transactions or none of them, ensuring that the data is updated in a consistent and predictable manner.

Conclusion

By following the best practices outlined in this article, developers can avoid common vulnerabilities in Solidity and write secure smart contracts. It is important to keep in mind that these vulnerabilities are just a few of the many that can occur in Solidity, and it is always a good idea to review your code and test it thoroughly to ensure that it is as secure as possible.

Exercises

To review these concepts, we will go through a series of exercises designed to test your understanding and apply what you have learned.

Write a function that takes two integers as arguments and adds them together, using the "SafeMath" library to prevent integer overflow.
Write a function that takes an integer as an argument and checks if it is within the range of 0 to 100.
Write a contract that has a public integer variable "counter" and a function "incrementCounter"

that increments the counter by 1. Use the "lock" pattern to prevent reentrancy.

Write a contract that has a public mapping of integers to strings and a function "setValue" that sets the value of a given key in the mapping. Use the "check-effects-interactions" pattern to prevent reentrancy.

Write a contract that has a public variable "balance" and a function "transfer" that transfers value from the contract to another contract or external address. Use the "require" function to check the return value of the "send" function and ensure that it was successful.

Solutions

Write a function that takes two integers as arguments and adds them together, using the "SafeMath" library to prevent integer overflow.

```
function add(uint x, uint y) public {
require(x + y >= x, "Integer overflow detected");
result = x + y;
}
```

Write a function that takes an integer as an argument and checks if it is within the range of 0 to 100.

```
function checkRange(uint x) public {
require(x >= 0 && x <= 100, "Integer not within range");
}
```

Write a contract that has a public integer variable "counter" and a function "incrementCounter" that increments the counter by 1. Use the "lock" pattern to prevent reentrancy.

```
pragma solidity ^0.5.0;
contract Counter {
bool public lock;
uint public counter;
function incrementCounter() public {
require(!lock, "Contract is currently locked");
lock = true;
counter++;
lock = false;
}
}
```

Write a contract that has a public mapping of integers to strings and a function "setValue" that sets the value of a given key in the mapping. Use the "check-effects-interactions" pattern to prevent reentrancy.

```
pragma solidity ^0.5.0;
```

```
contract Mapping {
 mapping(uint => string) public values;
 function setValue(uint key, string value) public {
  require(values[key] == "", "Key already has a value");
  values[key] = value;
 }
}
```

Write a contract that has a public variable "balance" and a function "transfer" that transfers value from the contract to another contract or external address. Use the "require" function to check the return value of the "send" function and ensure that it was successful.

```
pragma solidity ^0.5.0;
contract Transfer {
 uint public balance;
 function transfer(address recipient, uint amount) public {
  require(balance >= amount, "Insufficient balance");
  require(recipient.send(amount), "Transfer failed");
  balance -= amount;
 }
}
```

BEST PRACTICES FOR WRITING SECURE SMART CONTRACTS

Writing secure smart contracts is essential for ensuring the integrity and reliability of the Ethereum network and the applications built on it. In this article, we will discuss best practices for writing secure smart contracts in Solidity, the programming language used to write smart contracts on Ethereum.

Use Established Libraries and Frameworks

One of the best ways to ensure the security of your smart contracts is to use established libraries and frameworks that have been thoroughly tested and reviewed by the community. Some examples of popular libraries and frameworks include:

- OpenZeppelin: a collection of Solidity contracts and libraries for secure smart contract development.
- Truffle: a development framework for Ethereum that includes a library of tested contracts and a testing environment.
- Mythril: a security analysis tool that helps developers identify vulnerabilities in their smart contracts.

Follow the Principle of Least Privilege

The principle of least privilege states that a user or process should only have the minimum permissions necessary to perform its intended tasks. This is especially important in the context of smart contracts, as giving a contract too much access can make it vulnerable to attack.

To follow the principle of least privilege in your smart contracts, consider the following best practices:

- Use "view" functions whenever possible to allow external users to read data from the contract without modifying it.
- Use "onlyOwner" or similar modifiers to restrict the ability to modify contract state or execute certain functions to the contract owner or a specific group of users.
- Avoid using the "unrestricted" or "public" visibility specifiers unless absolutely necessary.

Test Thoroughly

Testing is crucial for ensuring the reliability and security of your smart contracts. It is important to test your contracts at every stage of development, from writing unit tests to testing on a test network before deploying to the main network.

Some best practices for testing smart contracts include:

- Write unit tests to test individual functions and contract behavior in isolation.
- Use a test network like Rinkeby or Ropsten to test your contracts in a simulated environment before deploying to the main network.
- Use a tool like Mythril to perform security analysis on your contracts and identify potential vulnerabilities.

Write Secure Code

Finally, it is important to follow best practices for writing secure code in general when writing smart contracts. This includes things like:

- Using the "SafeMath" library to prevent integer overflow and underflow.
- Avoiding reentrancy vulnerabilities by using the "lock" or "check-effects-interactions" patterns.
- Checking the return value of the "send" function to ensure that value transfers are successful.

Conclusion

By following these best practices, developers can write secure and reliable smart contracts that are resistant to vulnerabilities and attacks. It is important to keep in mind that security is an ongoing process, and it is important to continuously review and test your contracts to ensure that they are as secure as possible.

Exercises

To review these concepts, we will go through a series of exercises designed to test your understanding and apply what you have learned.

Write a contract that has a public integer variable "counter" and a function "incrementCounter" that increments the counter by 1. Use the "lock" pattern to prevent reentrancy.

Write a contract that has a public mapping of integers to strings and a function "setValue" that sets the value of a given key in the mapping. Use the "check-effects-interactions" pattern to prevent reentrancy.

Write a contract that has a public variable "balance" and a function "transfer" that transfers value from the contract to another contract or external address. Use the "require" function to check the return value of the "send" function and ensure that it was successful.

Write a function that takes two integers as arguments and adds them together, using the "SafeMath" library to prevent integer overflow.

Write a function that takes an integer as an argument and checks if it is within the range of 0 to 100.

Solutions

Write a contract that has a public integer variable "counter" and a function "incrementCounter" that increments the counter by 1. Use the "lock" pattern to prevent reentrancy.

```
pragma solidity ^0.5.0;
```

```solidity
contract Counter {
 bool public lock;
 uint public counter;
 function incrementCounter() public {
  require(!lock, "Contract is currently locked");
  lock = true;
  counter++;
  lock = false;
 }
}
```

Write a contract that has a public mapping of integers to strings and a function "setValue" that sets the value of a given key in the mapping. Use the "check-effects-interactions" pattern to prevent reentrancy.

```solidity
pragma solidity ^0.5.0;
contract Mapping {
 mapping(uint => string) public values;
 function setValue(uint key, string value) public {
  require(values[key] == "", "Key already has a value");
  values[key] = value;
 }
}
```

Write a contract that has a public variable "balance" and a function "transfer" that transfers value from the contract to another contract or external address. Use the "require" function to check the return value of the "send" function and ensure that it was successful.

```solidity
pragma solidity ^0.5.0;
contract Transfer {
 uint public balance;
 function transfer(address recipient, uint amount) public {
  require(balance >= amount, "Insufficient balance");
  require(recipient.send(amount), "Transfer failed");
  balance -= amount;
 }
}
```

Write a function that takes two integers as arguments and adds them together, using the "SafeMath" library to prevent integer overflow.

```solidity
function add(uint x, uint y) public {
```

```
require(x + y >= x, "Integer overflow detected");
result = x + y;
}
```

Write a function that takes an integer as an argument and checks if it is within the range of 0 to 100.

```
function checkRange(uint x) public {
require(x >= 0 && x <= 100, "Integer not within range");
}
```

WHAT ARE SOLIDITY LIBRARIES?

Solidity libraries are reusable code modules that can be called from within a Solidity contract. They are an important tool for developers who want to write efficient and maintainable smart contracts on the Ethereum platform. In this article, we will explore what Solidity libraries are, how they are used, and the benefits of using them.

What is a Solidity Library?

A Solidity library is a type of contract that contains a collection of functions that can be called from within other contracts. These functions are usually related to a specific task or set of tasks, such as arithmetic operations, string manipulation, or cryptographic functions.

Unlike regular contracts, Solidity libraries do not have their own storage or state. They are simply a way of packaging reusable code in a way that can be easily shared and imported into other contracts.

How are Solidity Libraries Used?

Solidity libraries are used to reduce code duplication and increase code reuse. For example, if you have a contract that needs to perform a series of arithmetic operations, you could write a library to contain those operations and then call the functions from within your contract. This would save you from having to write the same code multiple times, and it would make it easier to maintain the code in the future.

To use a Solidity library, you first need to import it into your contract using the "import" keyword. For example:

```
import "./MyLibrary.sol";
```

Once the library is imported, you can call its functions from within your contract by using the "libraryName.functionName" syntax. For example:

```
function add(uint x, uint y) public returns (uint) {
  return MyLibrary.add(x, y);
}
```

Benefits of Using Solidity Libraries

There are several benefits to using Solidity libraries:

- Code reuse: As mentioned above, libraries allow you to reuse code across multiple contracts, saving you from having to write the same code multiple times.
- Maintainability: By separating reusable code into libraries, you can make it easier to

maintain and update your codebase.
- Readability: By using libraries, you can make your contracts more readable and easier to understand by breaking complex tasks into smaller, more focused functions.
- Security: By using established libraries with a track record of security and reliability, you can reduce the risk of vulnerabilities in your contracts.

Conclusion

Solidity libraries are a powerful tool for developers who want to write efficient and maintainable smart contracts on the Ethereum platform. By allowing for code reuse, increased maintainability, and improved readability, libraries can help developers build better contracts and reduce the risk of vulnerabilities.

Exercises

To review these concepts, we will go through a series of exercises designed to test your understanding and apply what you have learned.

Write a Solidity library that contains a function to calculate the factorial of a given integer.

Write a Solidity library that contains a function to calculate the Fibonacci sequence up to a given integer.

Write a Solidity contract that imports the Fibonacci library and uses it to calculate the Fibonacci sequence up to a given integer.

Write a Solidity library that contains a function to calculate the GCD (greatest common divisor) of two integers.

Write a Solidity contract that imports the GCD library and uses it to calculate the GCD of two integers.

Solutions

Write a Solidity library that contains a function to calculate the factorial of a given integer.

```solidity
pragma solidity ^0.5.0;

library Factorial {
    function factorial(uint x) public pure returns (uint) {
        if (x == 0) {
            return 1;
        }
        return x * factorial(x - 1);
    }
}
```

Write a Solidity library that contains a function to calculate the Fibonacci sequence up to a given integer.

```solidity
pragma solidity ^0.5.0;

library Fibonacci {
```

```solidity
function fibonacci(uint x) public pure returns (uint) {
  if (x == 0) {
    return 0;
  }
  if (x == 1) {
    return 1;
  }
  return fibonacci(x - 1) + fibonacci(x - 2);
  }
}
```

Write a Solidity contract that imports the Fibonacci library and uses it to calculate the Fibonacci sequence up to a given integer.

```solidity
pragma solidity ^0.5.0;
import "./Fibonacci.sol";
contract FibonacciCalculator {
  function calculateFibonacci(uint x) public view returns (uint) {
    return Fibonacci.fibonacci(x);
  }
}
```

Write a Solidity library that contains a function to calculate the GCD (greatest common divisor) of two integers.

```solidity
pragma solidity ^0.5.0;
library GCD {
  function gcd(uint x, uint y) public pure returns (uint) {
    if (y == 0) {
      return x;
    }
    return gcd(y, x % y);
  }
}
```

Write a Solidity contract that imports the GCD library and uses it to calculate the GCD of two integers.

```solidity
pragma solidity ^0.5.0;
import "./GCD.sol";
contract GCDCalculator {
```

```
function calculateGCD(uint x, uint y) public view returns (uint) {
  return GCD.gcd(x, y);
}
}
```

HOW TO USE SOLIDITY LIBRARIES

Solidity libraries are a powerful tool for developers who want to write efficient and maintainable smart contracts on the Ethereum platform. In this article, we will explore how to use Solidity libraries in your own contracts and the benefits of doing so.

What is a Solidity Library?

A Solidity library is a type of contract that contains a collection of functions that can be called from within other contracts. These functions are usually related to a specific task or set of tasks, such as arithmetic operations, string manipulation, or cryptographic functions.

Unlike regular contracts, Solidity libraries do not have their own storage or state. They are simply a way of packaging reusable code in a way that can be easily shared and imported into other contracts.

How to use Solidity Libraries

To use a Solidity library, you first need to import it into your contract using the "import" keyword. For example:

```
import "./MyLibrary.sol";
```

Once the library is imported, you can call its functions from within your contract by using the "libraryName.functionName" syntax. For example:

```
function add(uint x, uint y) public returns (uint) {
  return MyLibrary.add(x, y);
}
```

Benefits of Using Solidity Libraries

There are several benefits to using Solidity libraries:

- Code reuse: By using libraries, you can reuse code across multiple contracts, saving you from having to write the same code multiple times.
- Maintainability: By separating reusable code into libraries, you can make it easier to maintain and update your codebase.
- Readability: By using libraries, you can make your contracts more readable and easier to understand by breaking complex tasks into smaller, more focused functions.
- Security: By using established libraries with a track record of security and reliability, you can reduce the risk of vulnerabilities in your contracts.

Best Practices for Using Solidity Libraries

When using Solidity libraries, there are a few best practices to follow:

- Use established libraries: There are many Solidity libraries available, and it's a good idea to use ones that have been well-reviewed and tested by the community.
- Document your code: Make sure to include clear documentation for your library functions, including descriptions of what they do and how to use them.
- Test your code: As with any contract, it's important to thoroughly test your library code to ensure it's reliable and secure.

Conclusion

Solidity libraries are a powerful tool for developers who want to write efficient and maintainable smart contracts on the Ethereum platform. By allowing for code reuse, increased maintainability, and improved readability, libraries can help developers build better contracts and reduce the risk of vulnerabilities. By following best practices, such as using established libraries and thoroughly testing your code, you can ensure that your contracts are reliable and secure.

Exercises

To review these concepts, we will go through a series of exercises designed to test your understanding and apply what you have learned.

Write a Solidity contract that imports the Factorial library and uses it to calculate the factorial of a given integer.

Write a Solidity contract that imports the GCD library and uses it to calculate the LCM (least common multiple) of two integers.

Write a Solidity contract that imports the Prime library and uses it to check if a given integer is prime.

Write a Solidity contract that imports the Fibonacci library and uses it to generate the first n elements of the Fibonacci sequence.

Write a Solidity contract that imports the Factorial library and uses it to calculate the sum of the first n elements of the factorial sequence (1! + 2! + 3! + … + n!).

Solutions

Write a Solidity contract that imports the Factorial library and uses it to calculate the factorial of a given integer.

```solidity
pragma solidity ^0.5.0;
import "./Factorial.sol";
contract FactorialCalculator {
function calculateFactorial(uint x) public view returns (uint) {
  return Factorial.factorial(x);
}
}
```

Write a Solidity contract that imports the GCD library and uses it to calculate the LCM (least common multiple) of two integers.

```solidity
pragma solidity ^0.5.0;
```

```solidity
import "./GCD.sol";
contract LCMCalculator {
 function calculateLCM(uint x, uint y) public view returns (uint) {
  return (x * y) / GCD.gcd(x, y);
 }
}
```

Write a Solidity contract that imports the Prime library and uses it to check if a given integer is prime.

```solidity
pragma solidity ^0.5.0;
import "./Prime.sol";
contract PrimeChecker {
 function isPrime(uint x) public view returns (bool) {
  return Prime.isPrime(x);
 }
}
```

Write a Solidity contract that imports the Fibonacci library and uses it to generate the first n elements of the Fibonacci sequence.

```solidity
pragma solidity ^0.5.0;
import "./Fibonacci.sol";
contract FibonacciGenerator {
 function generateFibonacciSequence(uint n) public view returns (uint[] memory) {
  uint[] memory result = new uint[](n);
  for (uint i = 0; i < n; i++) {
   result[i] = Fibonacci.fibonacci(i);
  }
  return result;
 }
}
```

Write a Solidity contract that imports the Factorial library and uses it to calculate the sum of the first n elements of the factorial sequence (1! + 2! + 3! + ... + n!).

```solidity
pragma solidity ^0.5.0;
import "./Factorial.sol";
contract FactorialSumCalculator {
 function calculateFactorialSum(uint n) public view returns (uint) {
  uint result = 0;
```

```
for (uint i = 1; i <= n; i++) {
  result += Factorial.factorial(i);
}
return result;
}
}
```

WHAT ARE DESIGN PATTERNS?

Design patterns are a key concept in software engineering that can help developers write more efficient, maintainable, and scalable code. In this article, we will explore what design patterns are, how they can be used in Solidity, and some of the most common design patterns used in smart contract development.

What are Design Patterns?

A design pattern is a reusable solution to a commonly occurring problem in software design. They are not specific pieces of code, but rather general approaches to solving common problems that can be applied in different contexts.

Design patterns were first introduced in the field of software engineering in the book "Design Patterns: Elements of Reusable Object-Oriented Software" by Erich Gamma, Richard Helm, Ralph Johnson, and John Vlissides, also known as the "Gang of Four" (GoF). The GoF book describes 23 design patterns that can be used to solve common problems in software design, and these patterns have become widely adopted in the software industry.

There are three main types of design patterns: creational, structural, and behavioral. Creational patterns deal with object creation mechanisms, trying to create objects in a manner suitable to the situation. Structural patterns deal with object composition, creating relationships between objects to form larger structures. Behavioral patterns focus on communication between objects, what goes on between objects and how they operate together.

Design patterns can help developers write better code by providing a standardized way of approaching common problems. They also help to improve communication between developers by providing a common vocabulary for discussing software design.

Design Patterns in Solidity

Design patterns can be applied in any programming language, including Solidity. Some common design patterns in Solidity include:

- Factory pattern: This pattern allows for the creation of multiple instances of a contract, each with its own unique state. It can be used to create token contracts or other types of contracts that need to track individual instances.
- Singleton pattern: This pattern ensures that there is only one instance of a contract. It can be used to create contracts that track global state, such as a central bank contract.
- Observer pattern: This pattern allows contracts to subscribe to events emitted by other contracts. It can be used to implement decentralized exchanges or other types of

contracts that need to track events across multiple contracts.

Other common design patterns in Solidity include the state machine pattern, the mutex pattern, and the access control pattern.

Best Practices for Using Design Patterns in Solidity

When using design patterns in Solidity, it's important to follow best practices to ensure your code is efficient, maintainable, and scalable:

- Use established patterns: There are many design patterns available, and it's a good idea to use ones that have been well-reviewed and tested by the community.
- Document your code: Make sure to include clear documentation for your contract's design pattern, including descriptions of what it does and how to use it.
- Test your code: As with any contract, it's important to thoroughly test your code to ensure it's reliable and secure.

Conclusion

Design patterns are a key concept in software engineering that can help developers write more efficient, maintainable, and scalable code. By providing a standardized way of approaching common problems, design patterns can help improve communication between developers and reduce the risk of vulnerabilities in smart contracts. By following best practices, such as using established patterns and thoroughly testing your code, you can ensure that your contracts are reliable and secure.

Exercises

To review these concepts, we will go through a series of exercises designed to test your understanding and apply what you have learned.

Write a Solidity contract that uses the factory pattern to create multiple instances of a token contract.

Write a Solidity contract that uses the singleton pattern to create a central bank contract that tracks global state.

Write a Solidity contract that uses the observer pattern to allow multiple contracts to subscribe to events emitted by a contract.

Write a Solidity contract that uses the state machine pattern to track the current state of a contract and only allow certain actions to be performed based on that state.

Write a Solidity contract that uses the mutex pattern to ensure that only one contract can perform a critical action at a time.

Solutions

Write a Solidity contract that uses the factory pattern to create multiple instances of a token contract.

```
pragma solidity ^0.5.0;

contract TokenFactory {

  address[] public tokens;

  function createToken() public {
```

```solidity
    address newToken = new Token();
    tokens.push(newToken);
  }
}
contract Token {
  // Contract code goes here...
}
```

Write a Solidity contract that uses the singleton pattern to create a central bank contract that tracks global state.

```solidity
pragma solidity ^0.5.0;
contract CentralBank {
  address private _singletonAddress;
  uint private _totalSupply;
  function CentralBank() public {
    // Ensure there is only one instance of this contract
    require(_singletonAddress == address(0));
    _singletonAddress = address(this);
  }
  function totalSupply() public view returns (uint) {
    return _totalSupply;
  }
  function issue(uint amount) public {
    require(msg.sender == _singletonAddress);
    _totalSupply += amount;
  }
}
```

Write a Solidity contract that uses the observer pattern to allow multiple contracts to subscribe to events emitted by a contract.

```solidity
pragma solidity ^0.5.0;
contract EventEmitter {
  event Event(uint value);
  function emitEvent(uint value) public {
    emit Event(value);
  }
}
```

```
contract EventObserver {
  EventEmitter public emitter;
  function EventObserver(address emitterAddress) public {
    emitter = EventEmitter(emitterAddress);
  }

  function subscribe() public {
    emitter.onEvent(handleEvent);
  }

  function handleEvent(uint value) public {
    // Event handling code goes here...
  }
}
```

Write a Solidity contract that uses the state machine pattern to track the current state of a contract and only allow certain actions to be performed based on that state.

```
pragma solidity ^0.5.0;
enum State { Created, Active, Inactive }
contract StateMachine {
  State public currentState;
  function StateMachine() public {
    currentState = State.Created;
  }

  function activate() public {
    require(currentState == State.Created || currentState == State.Inactive);
    currentState = State.Active;
  }

  function deactivate() public {
    require(currentState == State.Active);
    currentState = State.Inactive;
  }
}
```

Write a Solidity contract that uses the mutex pattern to ensure that only one contract can perform a critical action at a time.

```
pragma solidity ^0.5.0;
contract Mutex {
  bool public lock;
```

```solidity
function performCriticalAction() public {
  require(!lock);
  lock = true;
  // Perform critical action here...
  lock = false;
}
}
```

COMMON SOLIDITY DESIGN PATTERNS

Design patterns are a common concept in software engineering that provide a standardized way of solving common problems. In the world of Solidity, design patterns are particularly important as they can help ensure the reliability and security of smart contracts. In this article, we'll explore some of the most common design patterns used in Solidity and how they can be applied to your smart contracts.

Factory Pattern

The factory pattern is a creational design pattern that allows you to create multiple instances of a contract. This can be useful when you want to create multiple instances of the same contract, each with its own unique state.

To implement the factory pattern in Solidity, you can create a factory contract that has a function to create new instances of a target contract. The factory contract can then store a list of all the created instances and provide a way to access them.

Here's an example of a factory contract that creates instances of a token contract:

```solidity
pragma solidity ^0.5.0;
contract TokenFactory {
  address[] public tokens;
  function createToken() public {
    address newToken = new Token();
    tokens.push(newToken);
  }
}
contract Token {
  // Contract code goes here...
}
```

Singleton Pattern

The singleton pattern is a creational design pattern that ensures that there is only one instance of a contract. This can be useful when you want to ensure that there is only one central contract that controls certain global state.

To implement the singleton pattern in Solidity, you can include a private variable in your contract that stores the address of the singleton instance. You can then check this variable in the contract's constructor to ensure that there isn't already an instance of the contract.

Here's an example of a singleton contract that tracks the total supply of a token:

```solidity
pragma solidity ^0.5.0;
contract CentralBank {
  address private _singletonAddress;
  uint private _totalSupply;
  function CentralBank() public {
    // Ensure there is only one instance of this contract
    require(_singletonAddress == address(0));
    _singletonAddress = address(this);
  }
  function totalSupply() public view returns (uint) {
    return _totalSupply;
  }
  function issue(uint amount) public {
    require(msg.sender == _singletonAddress);
    _totalSupply += amount;
  }
}
```

Observer Pattern

The observer pattern is a behavioral design pattern that allows multiple contracts to subscribe to events emitted by another contract. This can be useful when you want to allow multiple contracts to react to changes in another contract's state.

To implement the observer pattern in Solidity, you can create an event emitter contract that emits events and a separate event observer contract that listens for those events. The observer contract can then have a function to handle the events when they are emitted.

Here's an example of an event emitter contract and an event observer contract:

```solidity
pragma solidity ^0.5.0;
// Deploy an instance of the event emitter contract
EventEmitter emitter = new EventEmitter();
// Deploy an instance of the event observer contract, passing in the address of the event emitter contract
EventObserver observer = new EventObserver(emitter.address);
// Emit an event from the event emitter contract
```

```
emitter.emitEvent(123);
// The event observer contract will automatically handle the event
```

State Machine Pattern

The state machine pattern is a behavioral design pattern that allows a contract to have multiple states and transition between those states based on certain actions. This can be useful when you want to model complex behavior in your smart contracts.

To implement the state machine pattern in Solidity, you can create an enumeration of all the possible states and a private variable to store the current state. You can then include functions in the contract to transition between states based on certain conditions.

Here's an example of a state machine contract that has three states: created, active, and inactive. The contract has functions to activate and deactivate the contract based on its current state:

```solidity
pragma solidity ^0.5.0;
enum State { Created, Active, Inactive }
contract StateMachine {
 State private currentState;
 function StateMachine() public {
   currentState = State.Created;
 }
 function activate() public {
   require(currentState == State.Created || currentState == State.Inactive);
   currentState = State.Active;
 }
 function deactivate() public {
   require(currentState == State.Active);
   currentState = State.Inactive;
 }
}
```

Conclusion

In this article, we explored some of the most common design patterns used in Solidity. By using these design patterns in your smart contracts, you can ensure the reliability and security of your contracts and model complex behavior.

Exercises

To review these concepts, we will go through a series of exercises designed to test your understanding and apply what you have learned.

Implement a state machine contract that has three states: created, approved, and rejected. The

contract should have functions to approve and reject the contract based on its current state.

Write a contract that uses the observer pattern to listen for events emitted by another contract. The contract should have a function to handle the event and update a state variable based on the event data.

Write a contract that uses the factory pattern to create instances of another contract. The contract should have a function to create new instances and a mapping to store the addresses of the created instances.

Write a contract that uses the proxy pattern to delegate calls to another contract. The contract should have a function to set the address of the delegate contract and a fallback function to delegate calls to the delegate contract.

Write a contract that uses the singleton pattern to ensure there is only one instance of the contract. The contract should have a function to check if an instance already exists and a fallback function to create a new instance if one does not exist.

Solutions

Implement a state machine contract that has three states: created, approved, and rejected. The contract should have functions to approve and reject the contract based on its current state.

```solidity
pragma solidity ^0.5.0;
enum State { Created, Approved, Rejected }
contract StateMachine {
 State private currentState;
 function StateMachine() public {
  currentState = State.Created;
 }
 function approve() public {
  require(currentState == State.Created);
  currentState = State.Approved;
 }
 function reject() public {
  require(currentState == State.Created);
  currentState = State.Rejected;
 }
}
```

Write a contract that uses the observer pattern to listen for events emitted by another contract. The contract should have a function to handle the event and update a state variable based on the event data.

```solidity
pragma solidity ^0.5.0;
contract EventObserver {
 uint public eventCount;
```

```solidity
function handleEvent(uint value) public {
  eventCount++;
}
function updateState(uint newState) public {
  emit StateUpdated(newState);
}
event StateUpdated(uint newState);
}
contract EventEmitter {
EventObserver observer;
function EventEmitter(address _observerAddress) public {
  observer = EventObserver(_observerAddress);
}
function emitEvent(uint value) public {
  observer.handleEvent(value);
}
function updateState(uint newState) public {
  observer.updateState(newState);
}
}
```

Write a contract that uses the factory pattern to create instances of another contract. The contract should have a function to create new instances and a mapping to store the addresses of the created instances.

```solidity
pragma solidity ^0.5.0;
contract Factory {
 mapping(uint => address) public createdContracts;
 function createContract() public {
  uint id = createdContracts.length;
  createdContracts[id] = new MyContract();
 }
}
contract MyContract {
uint public id;
function MyContract() public {
 id = msg.sender.balance;
}
}
```

Write a contract that uses the proxy pattern to delegate calls to another contract. The contract should have a function to set the address of the delegate contract and a fallback function to delegate calls to the delegate contract.

```solidity
pragma solidity ^0.5.0;
contract Proxy {
 address public delegate;
 function setDelegate(address _delegate) public {
  delegate = _delegate;
 }
 function() external payable {
  delegate.call(msg.data);
 }
}
contract Delegate {
 function doSomething() public {
  // Do something
 }
}
```

Write a contract that uses the singleton pattern to ensure there is only one instance of the contract. The contract should have a function to check if an instance already exists and a fallback function to create a new instance if one does not exist.

```solidity
pragma solidity ^0.5.0;
contract Singleton {
 address public instance;
 function checkInstance() public view returns (bool) {
  return address(this).balance > 0;
 }
 function() external payable {
  require(checkInstance() == false);
  instance = msg.sender;
 }
}
```

WHY IS TESTING IMPORTANT?

As a Solidity developer, it is crucial to thoroughly test your smart contracts to ensure they are functioning as intended. This is especially important when working with smart contracts on the Ethereum network, as these contracts are immutable and cannot be changed once deployed.

Ensuring Security

One of the main reasons testing is so important is to ensure the security of your smart contracts. Smart contracts handle valuable assets and it is essential that they are free from vulnerabilities that could potentially lead to the loss of these assets. Testing allows you to uncover any potential security issues and fix them before your contracts are deployed on the mainnet.

Ensuring Reliability and Correctness

In addition to security, testing also helps to ensure the reliability and correctness of your smart contracts. By thoroughly testing your contracts, you can catch any bugs or issues that may cause your contracts to malfunction. This is especially important when working with complex contracts that may have multiple interactions and dependencies.

Improving Maintainability

Testing also helps to improve the maintainability of your contracts. By writing comprehensive test cases, you can more easily understand the functionality of your contracts and make changes to them as needed. This can save time and effort in the long run, as you will have a better understanding of how your contracts work and how to troubleshoot any issues that may arise.

Conclusion

Overall, testing is an essential part of Solidity development and should not be overlooked. By taking the time to thoroughly test your contracts, you can ensure the security, reliability, and maintainability of your smart contracts and protect the valuable assets they handle.

Exercises

To review these concepts, we will go through a series of exercises designed to test your understanding and apply what you have learned.

Write a test case to ensure that a contract's function transfer(address _to, uint256 _value) **properly transfers the specified value to the specified address.**

Write a test case to ensure that a contract's function withdraw() **properly deducts the specified amount from the contract's balance and sends it to the caller.**

Write a test case to ensure that a contract's function addFunds() **properly adds the specified**

amount to the contract's balance and reduces the caller's balance by the same amount.

Write a test case to ensure that a contract's function executeTransaction(address _to, uint256 _value) **properly transfers the specified value to the specified address if the caller has provided the correct secret key.**

Write a test case to ensure that a contract's function executeTransaction(address _to, uint256 _value) **does not transfer the specified value if the caller has provided an incorrect secret key.**

Solutions

Write a test case to ensure that a contract's function transfer(address _to, uint256 _value) **properly transfers the specified value to the specified address.**

```solidity
pragma solidity ^0.5.0;
import "truffle/Assert.sol";
import "truffle/DeployedAddresses.sol";
import "../contracts/MyContract.sol";
contract TestMyContract {
 MyContract contract;
 function testTransfer() public {
   address receiver = 0x123456;
   uint value = 100;
   uint initialBalance = receiver.balance;
   contract.transfer(receiver, value);
   Assert.equal(receiver.balance, initialBalance + value, "Transfer failed");
 }
}
```

Write a test case to ensure that a contract's function withdraw()**properly deducts the specified amount from the contract's balance and sends it to the caller.**

```solidity
pragma solidity ^0.5.0;
import "truffle/Assert.sol";
import "truffle/DeployedAddresses.sol";
import "../contracts/MyContract.sol";
contract TestMyContract {
 MyContract contract;
 function testWithdraw() public {
   uint value = 100;
   uint initialBalance = contract.balance;
   uint initialCallerBalance = msg.sender.balance;
   contract.withdraw(value);
```

```
    Assert.equal(contract.balance, initialBalance - value, "Withdraw failed");
    Assert.equal(msg.sender.balance, initialCallerBalance + value, "Withdraw failed");
  }
}
```

Write a test case to ensure that a contract's function addFunds()**properly adds the specified amount to the contract's balance and reduces the caller's balance by the same amount.**

```
pragma solidity ^0.5.0;
import "truffle/Assert.sol";
import "truffle/DeployedAddresses.sol";
import "../contracts/MyContract.sol";
contract TestMyContract {
 MyContract contract;
 function testAddFunds() public {
  uint value = 100;
  uint initialContractBalance = contract.balance;
  uint initialCallerBalance = msg.sender.balance;
  contract.addFunds(value);
  Assert.equal(contract.balance, initialContractBalance + value, "Add funds failed");
  Assert.equal(msg.sender.balance, initialCallerBalance - value, "Add funds failed");
 }
}
```

Write a test case to ensure that a contract's function executeTransaction(address _to, uint256 _value) **properly transfers the specified value to the specified address if the caller has provided the correct secret key.**

```
pragma solidity ^0.5.0;
import "truffle/Assert.sol";
import "truffle/DeployedAddresses.sol";
import "../contracts/MyContract.sol";
contract TestMyContract {
 MyContract contract;
 function testExecuteTransaction() public {
  address receiver = 0x123456;
  uint value = 100;
  uint initialBalance = receiver.balance;
  bytes32 secretKey = "correctKey";
  contract.executeTransaction(receiver, value, secretKey);
```

```
Assert.equal(receiver.balance, initialBalance + value, "Transaction execution failed");
  }
}
```

Write a test case to ensure that a contract's function executeTransaction(address _to, uint256 _value) does not transfer the specified value if the caller has provided an incorrect secret key.

```
pragma solidity ^0.5.0;
import "truffle/Assert.sol";
import "truffle/DeployedAddresses.sol";
import "../contracts/MyContract.sol";
contract TestMyContract {
 MyContract contract;
 function testExecuteTransaction() public {
  address receiver = 0x123456;
  uint value = 100;
  uint initialBalance = receiver.balance;
  bytes32 secretKey = "incorrectKey";
  contract.executeTransaction(receiver, value, secretKey);
  Assert.equal(receiver.balance, initialBalance, "Transaction execution should have failed");
 }
}
```

SETTING UP A TESTING ENVIRONMENT

One of the key aspects of developing smart contracts is ensuring that they are robust and free of bugs. This is especially important given that once deployed, the code of a smart contract is immutable and cannot be changed. Therefore, it is essential to thoroughly test smart contracts before deploying them to a live network. In this chapter, we will cover how to set up a testing environment for Solidity contracts.

Setting up Truffle

Truffle is a popular development framework for Ethereum that includes a suite of tools for testing and debugging smart contracts. To get started with Truffle, you will need to have Node.js and npm installed on your machine. Once these dependencies are installed, you can install Truffle using npm:

```
npm install -g truffle
```

With Truffle installed, you can create a new project by running the following command:

```
truffle init
```

This will create a new directory with the following structure:

```
├── contracts
├── migrations
├── test
├── truffle-config.js
└── truffle.js
```

The contracts directory is where you will place your Solidity contract files. The migrations directory is used to manage the deployment of your contracts. The testdirectory is where you will place your test files. The truffle-config.js file is used to configure Truffle. The truffle.js file is used to specify the network you want to deploy to.

Setting up a TestRPC

TestRPC is a Node.js based Ethereum client for testing purposes. It provides an in-memory blockchain that can be used for testing without the need to connect to a live network. To install TestRPC, run the following command:

```
npm install -g ethereumjs-testrpc
```

Once installed, you can start a TestRPC instance by running the following command:

```
testrpc
```

This will start a TestRPC instance with 10 accounts and private keys, all with a balance of 100 ether. You can specify the number of accounts and the starting balance by passing in arguments:

```
testrpc --accounts 20 --balance 1000
```

Connecting Truffle to TestRPC

To connect Truffle to TestRPC, you will need to update the truffle.js file with the following configuration:

```
module.exports = {
 networks: {
  development: {
   host: "localhost",
   port: 8545,
   network_id: "*" // Match any network id
  }
 }
};
```

This will tell Truffle to connect to the TestRPC instance running on localhost on port 8545.

Running Tests

To run tests with Truffle, you can use the following command:

```
truffle test
```

This will run all the test files in the test directory. You can also specify a specific test file to run:

```
truffle test test/MyTest.sol
```

Conclusion:

In this chapter, we covered how to set up a testing environment for Solidity contracts using Truffle and TestRPC. We also covered how to run tests with Truffle.

Exercises

To review these concepts, we will go through a series of exercises designed to test your understanding and apply what you have learned.

What is the purpose of Truffle?
What is TestRPC and what is it used for?
How do you create a new Truffle project?
How do you start a TestRPC instance with 20 accounts and a starting balance of 1000 ether?

How do you run a specific test file with Truffle?

Solutions

What is the purpose of Truffle?
Truffle is a popular development framework for Ethereum that includes a suite of tools for testing and debugging smart contracts.

What is TestRPC and what is it used for?
TestRPC is a Node.js based Ethereum client for testing purposes. It provides an in-memory blockchain that can be used for testing without the need to connect to a live network.

How do you create a new Truffle project?
To create a new Truffle project, run the following command: truffle init.

How do you start a TestRPC instance with 20 accounts and a starting balance of 1000 ether?
To start a TestRPC instance with 20 accounts and a starting balance of 1000 ether, run the following command: testrpc --accounts 20 --balance 1000.

How do you run a specific test file with Truffle?
To run a specific test file with Truffle, use the following command: truffle test test/MyTest.sol.

WRITING TESTS FOR SOLIDITY CONTRACTS

Testing is an important aspect of developing smart contracts in Solidity. It helps ensure that your contracts are working as intended and can handle various scenarios and edge cases. In this chapter, we will learn how to write tests for Solidity contracts using Truffle and TestRPC.

What are Truffle and TestRPC?

Truffle is a popular development framework for Ethereum that includes a suite of tools for testing and debugging smart contracts. TestRPC is a Node.js based Ethereum client for testing purposes. It provides an in-memory blockchain that can be used for testing without the need to connect to a live network.

Setting Up a Testing Environment

To set up a testing environment for Solidity contracts, you will need to install Truffle and TestRPC. To install Truffle, run the following command:

```
npm install -g truffle
```

To install TestRPC, run the following command:

```
npm install -g ethereumjs-testrpc
```

Once both Truffle and TestRPC are installed, you can create a new Truffle project by running the following command:

```
truffle init
```

This will create a new directory with the following structure:

```
├── contracts
├── migrations
├── test
└── truffle.js
```

The contracts directory is where you will place your Solidity contracts. The migrations directory is where you will place your migration scripts. The testdirectory is where you will place your test files. The truffle.js file is the Truffle configuration file.

To start a TestRPC instance, run the following command:

```
testrpc
```

This will start an instance of TestRPC with 10 accounts and a starting balance of 100 ether. You can also specify the number of accounts and starting balance by using the --accounts and --balance flags. For example, to start a TestRPC instance with 20 accounts and a starting balance of 1000 ether, run the following command:

```
testrpc --accounts 20 --balance 1000
```

Writing Tests

To write tests for a Solidity contract, you will need to create a test file in the testdirectory. The test file should have a .js extension and should contain your test cases.

Here is an example of a test file for a simple contract called MyContract:

```
var MyContract = artifacts.require("MyContract");
contract("MyContract", function(accounts) {
it("should set the value to 5", function() {
  return MyContract.deployed().then(function(instance) {
    instance.setValue(5);
    return instance.getValue.call();
  }).then(function(value) {
    assert.equal(value, 5, "The value was not set to 5");
  });
});
});
```

This test case tests the setValue and getValue functions of the MyContractcontract. It deploys an instance of the contract, calls the setValue function with the value 5, and then calls the getValue function to retrieve the value. Finally, it asserts that the value returned by the getValue function is equal to 5.

Running Tests

To run the tests, you will need to have a TestRPC instance running in the background. Once the TestRPC instance is running, you can run the tests by using the following command:

```
truffle test
```

This will run all the test files in the test directory and display the results.

Advanced Testing Techniques

There are several advanced techniques that you can use when writing tests for Solidity contracts. Here are a few examples:

- Mocking external calls: If your contract makes calls to external contracts or APIs, you can use mock libraries like truffle-contract-mock to mock these calls and test the contract in isolation.
- Testing reverts: You can use the assert.throws function to test that a contract function reverts as expected in certain situations.
- Testing events: You can use the MyContract.deployed().then(function(instance) { instance.MyEvent().watch(function(error, result) { /* code */ });}); syntax to watch for events and test that they are emitted as expected.

Conclusion

In this chapter, we learned how to set up a testing environment for Solidity contracts using Truffle and TestRPC, and how to write test cases for Solidity contracts. Testing is an important aspect of developing smart contracts and can help ensure that your contracts are working as intended.

Exercises

To review these concepts, we will go through a series of exercises designed to test your understanding and apply what you have learned.

Write a test case for a contract that has a function that adds two numbers and returns the result.
Write a test case for a contract that has a function that reverts if the input is greater than 10.
Write a test case for a contract that has an event that is emitted when the value is changed.
Write a test case for a contract that makes a call to an external contract and tests that the call was made correctly.
Write a test case for a contract that has a function that takes a string as input and reverts if the string is empty.

Solutions

Write a test case for a contract that has a function that adds two numbers and returns the result.

```
it("should add two numbers and return the result", function() {
  return MyContract.deployed().then(function(instance) {
    return instance.addNumbers(5, 7).then(function(result) {
      assert.equal(result, 12, "The result was not correct");
    });
  });
});
```

Write a test case for a contract that has a function that reverts if the input is greater than 10.

```
it("should revert if the input is greater than 10", function() {
  return MyContract.deployed().then(function(instance) {
    return assert.throws(instance.revertIfGreaterThanTen(11));
  });
});
```

Write a test case for a contract that has an event that is emitted when the value is changed.

```
it("should emit the ValueChanged event when the value is changed", function() {
return MyContract.deployed().then(function(instance) {
 var eventWatcher = instance.ValueChanged();
 return instance.changeValue(5).then(function() {
  return eventWatcher.get();
 }).then(function(events) {
  assert.equal(events[0].args.newValue, 5, "The new value was not correct");
 });
 });
});
```

Write a test case for a contract that makes a call to an external contract and tests that the call was made correctly.

```
it("should make a call to an external contract and test that the call was made correctly", function() {
return MyContract.deployed().then(function(instance) {
 var mockExternalContract = sinon.mock(ExternalContract.at(instance.address));
 mockExternalContract.expects("someFunction").once().withArgs(5).returns(10);
 return instance.callExternalContract(5).then(function(result) {
  assert.equal(result, 10, "The result was not correct");
  mockExternalContract.verify();
 });
 });
});
```

Write a test case for a contract that has a function that takes a string as input and reverts if the string is empty.

```
it("should revert if the input string is empty", function() {
return MyContract.deployed().then(function(instance) {
  return assert.throws(instance.revertIfEmpty(""));
 });
});
```

ADVANCED DATA STRUCTURES

As you continue to develop smart contracts in Solidity, you will encounter situations where you need to store more complex data structures than simple variables and arrays. In this chapter, we will cover advanced data structures such as mappings, structs, and enums, which can be used to organize and manage your contract data more efficiently.

Mappings

Mappings are a data type in Solidity that allow you to store a value at a given key and retrieve it later. They are similar to hashes or dictionaries in other programming languages. Mappings are declared using the following syntax:

```
mapping(keyType => valueType) name;
```

For example, to declare a mapping that stores string values at address keys, you would write:

```
mapping(address => string) public userNames;
```

To set a value in a mapping, you can use the following syntax:

```
name[key] = value;
```

For example, to set a user's name in the above mapping, you could do the following:

```
userNames[msg.sender] = "Alice";
```

To retrieve a value from a mapping, you can use the same syntax:

```
value = name[key];
```

For example, to get a user's name from the above mapping, you could do the following:

```
string userName = userNames[msg.sender];
```

It's important to note that mappings are not iterable, meaning you cannot loop through the keys or values in a mapping. If you need to iterate through a mapping, you can use a data structure like an array to store the keys and then iterate through that.

Structs

Structs are a data type in Solidity that allow you to group multiple variables together into a single compound data type. They are similar to classes or objects in other programming languages. Structs are declared using the following syntax:

```
struct Name {
```

```
type1 var1;
type2 var2;
...
}
```

For example, to declare a struct to store a user's name and age, you could write:

```
struct User {
  string name;
  uint age;
}
```

To create a new instance of a struct, you can use the following syntax:

```
Name varName = Name(val1, val2, ...);
```

For example, to create a new User struct with the name "Alice" and age 25, you could do the following:

```
User alice = User("Alice", 25);
```

To access the variables in a struct, you can use the dot notation:

```
varName.var;
```

For example, to get the name of the above User struct, you could do the following:

```
string name = alice.name;
```

Enums

Enums are a great way to add meaning and context to your code by giving names to sets of related values. For example, you could use an enum to define the possible states of a task in a task management contract, like "TO_DO", "IN_PROGRESS", and "DONE".

To use an enum in your code, you can declare a variable of the enum type and assign it one of the constants. For example, to use the Days enum from the previous example:

```
Days today = Days.Monday;
```

You can also use enums in function arguments and return types, as well as in control structures like if statements. For example:

```
function getDayString(Days day) public pure returns (string) {
if (day == Days.Monday) {
  return "Monday";
} else if (day == Days.Tuesday) {
  return "Tuesday";
}
```

```
// ...
}
```

Enums are also useful for defining constants in your contract. For example, you could use an enum to define the possible values for a contract's state variable:

```
enum ContractState {
  INITIALIZED,
  ACTIVE,
  PAUSED,
  CLOSED
}
ContractState public state;
```

Conclusion

In conclusion, advanced data structures like mappings, structs, enums, and arrays are powerful tools for organizing and storing data in your Solidity contracts. By using these data structures, you can create complex and flexible contracts that can handle a wide range of scenarios. However, it's important to use these tools carefully and consider their performance and gas costs when designing your contracts.

Exercises

To review these concepts, we will go through a series of exercises designed to test your understanding and apply what you have learned.

Declare a mapping that stores uint values at address keys and assign it a name of your choosing.
Create a new instance of the User struct from the example above and assign it a name of your choosing.
Using the Days enum from the example above, declare a variable and assign it the value for Wednesday.
Write a function that takes a User struct as an argument and returns the user's name as a string.
Write a function that takes a ContractState enum as an argument and returns a string representation of the state. For example, if the input is ContractState.PAUSED, the function should return "Paused".

Solutions

Declare a mapping that stores uint values at address keys and assign it a name of your choosing.

```
mapping(address => uint) balances;
```

Create a new instance of the User struct from the example above and assign it a name of your choosing.

```
User myUser = User("Alice", 25);
```

Using the Days enum from the example above, declare a variable and assign it the value for Wednesday.

```
Days day = Days.Wednesday;
```

Write a function that takes a User struct as an argument and returns the user's name as a string.

```
function getUserName(User user) public pure returns (string) {
 return user.name;
}
```

Write a function that takes a ContractState enum as an argument and returns a string representation of the state. For example, if the input is ContractState.PAUSED, the function should return "Paused".

```
function getContractStateString(ContractState state) public pure returns (string) {
 if (state == ContractState.INITIALIZED) {
  return "Initialized";
 } else if (state == ContractState.ACTIVE) {
  return "Active";
 } else if (state == ContractState.PAUSED) {
  return "Paused";
 } else if (state == ContractState.CLOSED) {
  return "Closed";
 }
}
```

ADVANCED CONTRACT PATTERNS

As you become more comfortable with Solidity and smart contract development, you may find yourself wanting to use more advanced design patterns to build more complex and powerful contracts. In this chapter, we'll explore some common patterns that can help you take your contract development to the next level.

State Machines:

A state machine is a design pattern that allows you to model the different states that a contract can be in, and the transitions between those states. This can be especially useful for contracts that have complex logic or need to handle multiple scenarios.

To implement a state machine in Solidity, you'll need to define an enum that represents the different states that your contract can be in. You'll also need to define a state variable that stores the current state of the contract. Here's an example of a simple state machine contract:

```solidity
pragma solidity ^0.6.0;
enum ContractState {
  INITIALIZED,
  ACTIVE,
  PAUSED,
  CLOSED
}
ContractState public state;
function setState(ContractState _state) public {
  require(_state != state, "State is already set to this value");
  state = _state;
}
```

In this example, the contract has a state variable called state that can be one of four values: INITIALIZED, ACTIVE, PAUSED, or CLOSED. The setState function allows you to change the state of the contract, but only if the new state is different from the current state.

Dependency Injection:

Dependency injection is a design pattern that allows you to decouple different components of your contract by injecting their dependencies (e.g. other contracts or libraries) at runtime. This can make it easier to test your contracts and make changes to their dependencies without affecting the rest of the contract.

To use dependency injection in your Solidity contracts, you can define a contract interface that specifies the functions and variables that the dependency must implement, and then pass an instance of that dependency to your contract as a constructor argument. Here's an example of a contract that uses dependency injection:

```solidity
pragma solidity ^0.6.0;
interface Token {
 function balanceOf(address _owner) external view returns (uint);
 function transfer(address _to, uint _value) external;
}
contract MyContract {
 Token public token;
 constructor(Token _token) public {
  token = _token;
 }
 function transferTokens(address _to, uint _value) public {
  require(token.balanceOf(msg.sender) >= _value, "Not enough tokens");
  token.transfer(_to, _value);
 }
}
```

In this example, the MyContract contract depends on a contract that implements the Token interface. When an instance of MyContract is created, it receives an instance of the Token contract as a constructor argument. The MyContract contract can then use the token variable to call functions on the Token contract.

Circuit Breakers

Circuit breakers are a common pattern used in smart contracts to allow for emergency shutdowns in case of unexpected errors or attacks. They allow the contract owner or a designated authority to pause the contract's functions in order to fix any issues or vulnerabilities.

To implement a circuit breaker in Solidity, you can use a boolean flag to indicate whether the contract is paused or not. Then, you can use this flag to modify the behavior of your contract's functions. For example:

```solidity
pragma solidity ^0.6.0;
contract CircuitBreaker {
  bool public paused;
  constructor() public {
```

```solidity
        paused = false;
    }
    function pause() public {
        require(!paused, "The contract is already paused.");
        paused = true;
    }
    function unpause() public {
        require(paused, "The contract is not paused.");
        paused = false;
    }
    function doSomething() public {
        require(!paused, "The contract is paused.");
        // Do something
    }
}
```

In this example, the pause() function can be called by the contract owner or a designated authority to set the paused flag to true. The unpause() function can then be used to set the flag back to false. The doSomething() function is then modified to check the value of the paused flag before executing, ensuring that it cannot be called while the contract is paused.

It's important to note that circuit breakers should only be used as a last resort, as they can disrupt the normal operation of the contract. They should also be implemented with caution, as they can potentially be exploited if not implemented properly.

Upgradability:

One of the challenges of smart contract development is that once a contract is deployed to the Ethereum network, it's difficult to change. This can make it hard to fix bugs or add new features to your contracts.

To solve this problem, you can use the upgradability pattern to build contracts that can be easily updated without requiring a new deployment. There are several ways to implement upgradability in Solidity, but one common approach is to use a proxy contract that delegates calls to an implementation contract. The proxy contract can be updated to delegate calls to a new implementation contract, allowing you to make changes to the contract logic without affecting the contract's address or its stored data.

Here's an example of a simple proxy contract:

```solidity
pragma solidity ^0.6.0;
contract MyContract {
    function execute(bytes calldata _data) external;
```

```
}
contract MyContractProxy {
  MyContract public implementation;
  constructor(MyContract _implementation) public {
    implementation = _implementation;
  }
  function execute(bytes calldata _data) external {
    implementation.execute(_data);
  }
}
```

In this example, the MyContractProxy contract has a public variable called implementation that stores an instance of the MyContract contract. The executefunction simply delegates the call to the execute function of the implementationcontract. To update the contract, you would deploy a new instance of the MyContractcontract and set the implementation variable of the MyContractProxy contract to the new instance.

Delegation:

The delegation pattern allows you to delegate certain functions or responsibilities to another contract or address. This can be useful in situations where you want to outsource part of the contract logic to another contract, or allow a third party to perform certain actions on your behalf.

To implement delegation in Solidity, you can define a function that takes an address or contract as an argument and calls a function on that address or contract. Here's an example of a contract that uses delegation:

```
pragma solidity ^0.6.0;
contract MyContract {
  function execute(address _delegate, bytes calldata _data) external {
    require(_delegate.call(_data), "Delegate call failed");
  }
}
```

In this example, the execute function takes an address as an argument and calls the call function on that address, passing in the _data argument. This allows the contract to delegate the execution of the _data to the specified address.

Conclusion:

Using advanced design patterns like state machines, dependency injection, circuit breakers, upgradability, and delegation can help you build more robust and flexible smart contracts. While these patterns can be useful in certain situations, it's important to carefully consider their trade-offs and ensure that you are using them in a way that is appropriate for your specific use case.

Exercises

To review these concepts, we will go through a series of exercises designed to test your understanding and apply what you have learned.

Write a Solidity contract that includes a circuit breaker. The circuit breaker should have a pause() **function that can be called by the contract owner, and a** doSomething() **function that is modified to check the value of the circuit breaker before executing.**

Modify the contract from Exercise 1 to include an unpause() **function that can be called by the contract owner to set the circuit breaker back to** false.

Modify the contract from Exercise 2 to include a doSomethingElse()**function that is also modified to check the value of the circuit breaker before executing.**

Write a Solidity contract that implements a circuit breaker pattern. The contract should have a public function called emergencyShutdown**that sets a boolean value called** shutdown **to true. The contract should also have a public function called** resume **that sets the** shutdown **value to false. The contract should have a public function called** isShutdown **that returns the value of** shutdown.

Write a Solidity contract that uses a circuit breaker pattern to stop a function from being called if the shutdown **value is true. The contract should have a public function called** doImportantWork **that increments a value called** counter **by 1. The contract should have a public function called** getCounter **that returns the value of** counter.

Solutions

Write a Solidity contract that includes a circuit breaker. The circuit breaker should have a pause() **function that can be called by the contract owner, and a** doSomething() **function that is modified to check the value of the circuit breaker before executing.**

```solidity
pragma solidity ^0.6.0;
contract CircuitBreakerExercise {
  bool public paused;
  constructor() public {
    paused = false;
  }
  function pause() public {
    require(!paused, "The contract is already paused.");
    paused = true;
  }
  function doSomething() public {
    require(!paused, "The contract is paused.");
    // Do something
  }
}
```

Modify the contract from Exercise 1 to include an unpause() **function that can be called by the**

contract owner to set the circuit breaker back to false.

```solidity
pragma solidity ^0.6.0;
contract CircuitBreakerExercise {
  bool public paused;
  constructor() public {
    paused = false;
  }
  function pause() public {
    require(!paused, "The contract is already paused.");
    paused = true;
  }
  function unpause() public {
    require(paused, "The contract is not paused.");
    paused = false;
  }
  function doSomething() public {
    require(!paused, "The contract is paused.");
    // Do something
  }
}
```

Modify the contract from Exercise 2 to include a doSomethingElse()**function that is also modified to check the value of the circuit breaker before executing.**

```solidity
pragma solidity ^0.6.0;
contract CircuitBreakerExercise {
  bool public paused;
  constructor() public {
    paused = false;
  }
  function pause() public {
    require(!paused, "The contract is already paused.");
    paused = true;
  }
  function unpause() public {
    require(paused, "The contract is not paused.");
    paused = false;
  }
```

```solidity
function doSomething() public {
    require(!paused, "The contract is paused.");
    // Do something
}
function doSomethingElse() public {
    require(!paused, "The contract is paused.");
    // Do something else
}
}
```

Write a Solidity contract that implements a circuit breaker pattern. The contract should have a public function called emergencyShutdownthat sets a boolean value called shutdown to true. The contract should also have a public function called resume that sets the shutdown value to false. The contract should have a public function called isShutdown that returns the value of shutdown.

```solidity
pragma solidity ^0.7.0;
contract CircuitBreaker {
    bool public shutdown;
    function emergencyShutdown() public {
        shutdown = true;
    }
    function resume() public {
        shutdown = false;
    }
    function isShutdown() public view returns (bool) {
        return shutdown;
    }
}
```

Write a Solidity contract that uses a circuit breaker pattern to stop a function from being called if the shutdown value is true. The contract should have a public function called doImportantWork that increments a value called counter by 1. The contract should have a public function called getCounter that returns the value of counter.

```solidity
pragma solidity ^0.7.0;
contract CircuitBreaker {
    bool public shutdown;
    uint public counter;
    function doImportantWork() public {
        require(!shutdown, "The contract is in shutdown mode and cannot perform this action.");
```

```
    counter++;
  }
  function getCounter() public view returns (uint) {
    return counter;
  }
}
```

WORKING WITH ORACLE

Oracles are third-party services that provide external data to smart contracts on the blockchain. They are a crucial component in many decentralized applications (DApps), as they allow smart contracts to interact with the real world and make decisions based on external data. In this chapter, we will explore the different types of oracles and how to work with them in Solidity.

What are Oracles?

Oracles are services that bridge the gap between the blockchain and the real world. They provide smart contracts with access to external data, such as stock prices, weather data, and sporting event results. This enables smart contracts to make decisions based on real-world data and trigger actions in the real world, such as paying out insurance claims or executing a financial trade.

Oracles can be classified into two main categories:

1. **On-chain oracles:** These are smart contracts that are deployed on the same blockchain as the contract they are providing data to. They are typically called by the contract and return the requested data directly to it.
2. **Off-chain oracles:** These are external services that are not deployed on the blockchain. They provide data to smart contracts through an API or other means of communication.

Why use an Oracle?

There are several reasons why you might want to use an Oracle in a smart contract:

- To access data that is not stored on the blockchain
- To trigger a contract based on external events
- To verify the authenticity of external data

Types of Oracles

There are several types of oracles, each with its own unique characteristics and use cases. Some common types of oracles include:

1. **Software oracles:** These are oracles that provide data from software applications, such as stock prices from financial exchanges or weather data from meteorological agencies.
2. **Hardware oracles:** These are oracles that provide data from hardware sensors or devices, such as temperature readings from smart thermostats or traffic data from smart traffic lights.
3. **Human oracles:** These are oracles that provide data based on human input, such as sporting event results or election outcomes.
4. **Hybrid oracles:** These are oracles that combine elements from multiple oracle types, such as a smart contract that uses both software and hardware oracles to gather data.

Working with Oracles in Solidity

There are several ways to work with oracles in Solidity, depending on the type of oracle and the data being requested. Some common approaches include:

1. **Web3.js:** Web3.js is a JavaScript library that allows contracts to make calls to external APIs and receive data from off-chain oracles. Web3.js can be used in conjunction with HTTP, WebSockets, and other communication protocols to retrieve data from a variety of sources.
2. **Contract callbacks:** Many on-chain oracles expose a callback function that can be called by the contract to request data. The oracle then returns the data directly to the contract through the callback function.
3. **Event logging:** Some oracles log data to the blockchain as events, which can be listened for and parsed by the contract. This is a common approach for oracles that provide data on a regular basis, such as price feeds.

How to use an Oracle in Solidity

Using an Oracle in Solidity is relatively simple. First, you will need to find an Oracle service that provides the data you need. There are many Oracle services available, such as Oraclize and Chainlink.

Once you have chosen an Oracle service, you will need to integrate it into your smart contract. This will typically involve importing a library provided by the Oracle service and using their API to request data.

Here is an example of how to use the Oraclize Oracle in a Solidity contract:

```solidity
pragma solidity ^0.7.0;
import "https://github.com/oraclize/ethereum-api/oraclizeAPI.sol";
contract MyContract is usingOraclize {
  string public data;
  constructor() public {
    oraclize_setNetwork(networkID_ropsten);
  }
  function requestData() public {
    oraclize_query("URL", "json(https://api.example.com).data");
  }
  function __callback(bytes32 _queryId, string memory _result) public {
    data = _result;
  }
}
```

In this example, we are using the Oraclize API to request data from the "https://api.example.com" URL and storing the result in the data variable.

Conclusion

Oracles are an essential component of many decentralized applications, as they allow smart contracts to interact with the real world and make decisions based on external data. There are various types of oracles, including software, hardware, human, and hybrid oracles, and several approaches to working with them in Solidity. Understanding how to use oracles can greatly enhance the functionality and capabilities of your smart contracts.

Exercises

To review these concepts, we will go through a series of exercises designed to test your understanding and apply what you have learned.

Write a Solidity contract that sends a request to an Oracle to retrieve the current price of a given cryptocurrency. The contract should have a function called requestPrice **that takes in a string argument representing the cryptocurrency symbol (e.g. "BTC" for Bitcoin). The function should then call the Oracle with this symbol as a parameter and return the price in wei.**

Write a Solidity contract that allows users to place bets on the price of a cryptocurrency at a future date. The contract should have a function called placeBet **that takes in a string argument representing the cryptocurrency symbol (e.g. "BTC" for Bitcoin), a uint representing the amount of wei to bet, and a uint representing the timestamp of when the bet should be resolved. The function should then call the Oracle to retrieve the current price of the cryptocurrency and store it in a mapping. When the timestamp is reached, the contract should compare the current price of the cryptocurrency to the stored price and send the bet amount to the winner.**

Create a Solidity contract that listens for an external event with data about the current temperature in a particular city. Use an oracle service to retrieve the data and trigger the event.

Create a Solidity contract that allows users to place bets on the outcome of a sporting event. Use an oracle service to retrieve the final score and pay out the winners.

Create a smart contract that utilizes an oracle to get the current temperature in Fahrenheit for a given city. The contract should have a function that allows users to input a city name, and it should return the current temperature in Fahrenheit for that city.

Solutions

Write a Solidity contract that sends a request to an Oracle to retrieve the current price of a given cryptocurrency. The contract should have a function called requestPrice **that takes in a string argument representing the cryptocurrency symbol (e.g. "BTC" for Bitcoin). The function should then call the Oracle with this symbol as a parameter and return the price in wei.**

```solidity
pragma solidity ^0.7.0;

import "https://github.com/OpenZeppelin/openzeppelin-solidity/contracts/math/SafeMath.sol";

contract Oracle {

    function requestPrice(string memory symbol) public view returns (uint price);

}

contract CryptoPrice {

    using SafeMath for uint;
```

```solidity
Oracle oracle;
constructor(address _oracle) public {
    oracle = Oracle(_oracle);
}
function requestPrice(string memory symbol) public view returns (uint price) {
    return oracle.requestPrice(symbol);
}
}
```

Write a Solidity contract that allows users to place bets on the price of a cryptocurrency at a future date. The contract should have a function called placeBet that takes in a string argument representing the cryptocurrency symbol (e.g. "BTC" for Bitcoin), a uint representing the amount of wei to bet, and a uint representing the timestamp of when the bet should be resolved. The function should then call the Oracle to retrieve the current price of the cryptocurrency and store it in a mapping. When the timestamp is reached, the contract should compare the current price of the cryptocurrency to the stored price and send the bet amount to the winner.

```solidity
pragma solidity ^0.7.0;
import "https://github.com/OpenZeppelin/openzeppelin-solidity/contracts/math/SafeMath.sol";
contract Oracle {
    function requestPrice(string memory symbol) public view returns (uint price);
}
contract CryptoBet {
    using SafeMath for uint;
    Oracle oracle;
    mapping(string => uint) public betPrices;
    constructor(address _oracle) public {
        oracle = Oracle(_oracle);
    }
    function placeBet(string memory symbol, uint amount, uint timestamp) public payable {
        betPrices[symbol] = oracle.requestPrice(symbol);
        require(now <= timestamp, "Bet resolution time has already passed.");
        require(amount <= msg.value, "Bet amount must be equal to or greater than the value sent.");
        require(amount > 0, "Bet amount must be greater than 0.");
        uint currentPrice = oracle.requestPrice(symbol);
        if (currentPrice > betPrices[symbol]) {
            // bet was correct, send amount to winner
            msg.sender.transfer(amount);
        } else if (currentPrice < betPrices[symbol]) {
```

```
// bet was incorrect, send amount to contract owner
    address(owner).transfer(amount);
  }
  // bet was a tie, do nothing
  }
}
```

Create a Solidity contract that listens for an external event with data about the current temperature in a particular city. Use an oracle service to retrieve the data and trigger the event.

First, we need to define the event in our contract:

```
event NewTemperature(uint temperature);
```

Next, we will create a function that will be called by the oracle service to trigger the event:

```
function updateTemperature(uint _temperature) public {
  emit NewTemperature(_temperature);
}
```

To retrieve the temperature data from the oracle service, we will use the oraclize_query function. Here is an example of how to use it to get the current temperature in New York City:

```
oraclize_query("URL",                "json(http://api.openweathermap.org/data/2.5/weather?q=New
%20York,us).main.temp");
```

We can then parse the temperature data and call the updateTemperaturefunction to trigger the event:

```
function __callback(bytes32 _queryId, string _result) public {
  uint temperature = parseInt(_result, 0);
  updateTemperature(temperature);
}
```

Create a Solidity contract that allows users to place bets on the outcome of a sporting event. Use an oracle service to retrieve the final score and pay out the winners.

First, we will define a struct to represent a bet and an array to store all the bets:

```
struct Bet {
  uint amount;
  uint teamA;
  uint teamB;
}
Bet[] public bets;
```

Next, we will create a function for users to place their bets:

```solidity
function placeBet(uint _amount, uint _teamA, uint _teamB) public payable {
    require(msg.value == _amount, "Incorrect bet amount");
    bets.push(Bet(_amount, _teamA, _teamB));
}
```

To retrieve the final score from the oracle service, we can use the oraclize_query function in a similar way as in the previous exercise. Once we have the final score, we can iterate through the bets array and pay out the winners:

```solidity
function __callback(bytes32 _queryId, string _result) public {
    uint scoreA = parseInt(_result, 0);
    uint scoreB = parseInt(_result, 1);
    for (uint i = 0; i < bets.length; i++) {
        if (scoreA > scoreB && bets[i].teamA > bets[i].teamB) {
            msg.sender.transfer(bets[i].amount);
        } else if (scoreA < scoreB && bets[i].teamA < bets[i].teamB) {
            msg.sender.transfer(bets[i].amount);
        }
    }
}
```

Create a smart contract that utilizes an oracle to get the current temperature in Fahrenheit for a given city. The contract should have a function that allows users to input a city name, and it should return the current temperature in Fahrenheit for that city.

```solidity
pragma solidity ^0.6.0;
import "https://github.com/oraclize/ethereum-api/solidity/contracts/oraclizeAPI.sol";
// contract to get current temperature in Fahrenheit for a given city
contract TemperatureOracle {
    // variable to store the current temperature in Fahrenheit
    uint temperature;
    // event to be emitted when the temperature is updated
    event TemperatureUpdate(uint temperature);
    // constructor to set the oracle address
    constructor() public {
        oraclize_setProof(proofType_TLSNotary | proofStorage_IPFS);
    }
    // function to get the current temperature in Fahrenheit for a given city
    function getTemperature(string memory city) public {
```

```solidity
        // call the oracle to get the current temperature in Fahrenheit for the given city
        oraclize_query(60, "URL", "json(https://api.openweathermap.org/data/2.5/weather?q=" + city + "&units=imperial).main.temp");
    }

    // callback function to handle the response from the oracle
    function __callback(bytes32 queryId, string memory result, bytes memory proof) public {
        // parse the result string to extract the temperature in Fahrenheit
        temperature = uint(parseInt(result));
        // emit the TemperatureUpdate event
        emit TemperatureUpdate(temperature);
    }
}
```

REAL-WORLD EXAMPLES
OF SOLIDITY IN USE

In this chapter, we will explore some real-world examples of how Solidity is being used to build decentralized applications (DApps) on the Ethereum platform. Understanding how Solidity is used in real-world scenarios can help you get a better grasp of the capabilities of this programming language and inspire you to build your own DApps.

Cryptocurrency Exchanges

One common use case for Solidity is building cryptocurrency exchanges. A cryptocurrency exchange is a platform that allows users to buy and sell different types of cryptocurrencies, such as Bitcoin and Ethereum. These exchanges typically have a matching engine that matches buyers and sellers based on the price they are willing to pay or receive.

One example of a cryptocurrency exchange built using Solidity is 0x Protocol. 0x Protocol is an open-source protocol that allows for the decentralized exchange of Ethereum-based tokens. It utilizes a system of smart contracts to facilitate the exchange of tokens without the need for a centralized third party.

Supply Chain Management

Another area where Solidity is being used is in supply chain management. Supply chain management involves the planning, coordination, and control of the flow of goods, services, and information from the point of origin to the point of consumption.

One example of a DApp built using Solidity for supply chain management is Provenance. Provenance is a blockchain-based platform that helps companies track the origin, location, and movement of products as they move through the supply chain. By using smart contracts, Provenance allows companies to automate the tracking process and ensure the accuracy of the data.

Identity Verification

Identity verification is another use case for Solidity. Identity verification refers to the process of verifying the identity of an individual or organization. This is often necessary for financial transactions, opening bank accounts, or accessing certain services.

One example of a DApp built using Solidity for identity verification is uPort. uPort is a self-sovereign identity platform that allows individuals to own and control their own digital identity. It uses smart contracts to create a secure and decentralized system for identity verification.

Conclusion

These are just a few examples of how Solidity is being used to build real-world DApps. As the Ethereum platform and the use of smart contracts continue to grow, it is likely that we will see even more innovative and creative uses for Solidity.

Exercises

To review these concepts, we will go through a series of exercises designed to test your understanding and apply what you have learned.

Choose a real-world example of Solidity in use and explain how it is being used.

Choose a real-world example of Solidity in use and describe the benefits it brings to the application or platform.

Choose a real-world example of Solidity in use and discuss any challenges or limitations it faces.

Choose a real-world example of Solidity in use and discuss any security considerations that need to be taken into account.

Write a Solidity contract that represents a simple crowdfunding campaign. The contract should have the following features:

-A goal amount that the campaign is trying to raise

-A deadline for the campaign to reach its goal

-A method for contributors to donate Ether to the campaign

-A method for the campaign owner to withdraw any funds that have been raised if the goal has been reached before the deadline

-A method for contributors to retrieve their donations if the goal has not been reached by the deadline

Solutions

Choose a real-world example of Solidity in use and explain how it is being used.

One real-world example of Solidity in use is the Ethereum blockchain itself. Solidity is the primary programming language used to write smart contracts on Ethereum, and these smart contracts are used to facilitate a wide range of decentralized applications (DApps). Some examples of DApps built on Ethereum using Solidity include decentralized exchanges (DEXs), prediction markets, and peer-to-peer marketplaces. In these cases, Solidity is used to encode the rules and logic of the DApp, allowing it to operate in a transparent and trustless manner on the Ethereum network.

Choose a real-world example of Solidity in use and describe the benefits it brings to the application or platform.

One real-world example of Solidity in use is the Augur prediction market platform. Augur is a decentralized application (DApp) built on Ethereum that allows users to create and participate in prediction markets on a wide range of topics. By using Solidity to encode the rules and logic of the platform, Augur is able to operate in a transparent and trustless manner, without the need for a central authority or intermediaries. This not only helps to ensure the integrity and fairness of the platform, but also allows it to operate in a decentralized and censorship-resistant manner.

Choose a real-world example of Solidity in use and discuss any challenges or limitations it faces.

One real-world example of Solidity in use is the Cryptokitties platform. Cryptokitties is a decentralized application (DApp) built on Ethereum that allows users to buy, sell, and breed digital cats using smart contracts written in Solidity. While the use of Solidity has allowed Cryptokitties to operate in a transparent and trustless manner, it has also faced some challenges and limitations. For example, the Ethereum network can only process a limited number of transactions per second, which can lead to delays and high gas fees during periods of high demand. Additionally, the use of smart contracts can make it difficult to change or update the rules of the platform once they have been deployed, which can limit the ability of the Cryptokitties team to respond to changing market conditions or user needs.

Choose a real-world example of Solidity in use and discuss any security considerations that need to be taken into account.

One real-world example of Solidity in use is the MakerDAO decentralized finance (DeFi) platform. MakerDAO is a decentralized application (DApp) built on Ethereum that allows users to take out loans using cryptocurrency as collateral. The smart contracts that power the MakerDAO platform are written in Solidity, and these contracts are responsible for managing the collateral, issuing loans, and enforcing repayment terms. As such, it is important that these contracts are secure and free from vulnerabilities that could be exploited by malicious actors. Some potential security considerations for the MakerDAO platform include the need to carefully audit and test the smart contracts before deployment, the need to monitor the platform for potential vulnerabilities or attacks, and the need to have robust emergency measures in place to protect against potential losses or liquidations.

Write a Solidity contract that represents a simple crowdfunding campaign. The contract should have the following features:
-A goal amount that the campaign is trying to raise
-A deadline for the campaign to reach its goal
-A method for contributors to donate Ether to the campaign
-A method for the campaign owner to withdraw any funds that have been raised if the goal has been reached before the deadline
-A method for contributors to retrieve their donations if the goal has not been reached by the deadline

```solidity
pragma solidity ^0.6.0;
contract Crowdfunding {
    // The goal amount the campaign is trying to raise
    uint goal;
    // The deadline for the campaign to reach its goal
    uint deadline;
    // The amount of Ether that has been raised so far
    uint raised;
    // Mapping of contributors and their donations
    mapping(address => uint) public contributions;
    // The campaign owner
```

```solidity
address public owner;
constructor(uint _goal, uint _deadline) public {
    owner = msg.sender;
    goal = _goal;
    deadline = _deadline;
}
// Method for contributors to donate Ether to the campaign
function donate() public payable {
    require(now <= deadline, "Campaign deadline has passed");
    contributions[msg.sender] += msg.value;
    raised += msg.value;
}
// Method for the campaign owner to withdraw funds if the goal has been reached
function withdraw() public {
    require(raised >= goal, "Goal has not been reached");
    require(msg.sender == owner, "Only the owner can withdraw funds");
    owner.transfer(raised);
}
// Method for contributors to retrieve their donations if the goal has not been reached
function refund() public {
    require(now > deadline, "Campaign deadline has not passed");
    require(raised < goal, "Goal has been reached");
    uint refundAmount = contributions[msg.sender];
    contributions[msg.sender] = 0;
    msg.sender.transfer(refundAmount);
}
}
```

TIPS AND TRICKS FOR WORKING WITH SOLIDITY

In this chapter, we will be sharing some tips and tricks that we have learned while working with Solidity. These tips and tricks will help you to become more efficient and effective while working with Solidity.

Debugging

Debugging can be a challenging task when it comes to working with Solidity. However, there are a few tools and techniques that can make this process easier.

- One of the first things you should do when debugging your Solidity code is to enable debugging in your development environment. This will allow you to see the input and output of your contract at each step.
- Another helpful tip is to use the Solidity debugger. This tool allows you to step through your code line by line and see the values of variables at each step.
- It can also be helpful to add console logs to your code. This will allow you to see the values of variables and the output of your contract at each step.

Testing

Testing is an essential part of the development process when it comes to working with Solidity. Here are a few tips for writing effective tests:

- Make sure to test all of the functions in your contract. This includes both positive and negative test cases.
- Use a test coverage tool to ensure that you are testing all of the code in your contract.
- Use test-driven development (TDD) to write your tests before you write your code. This will help you to identify any potential issues early on in the development process.

Security

Security is a critical concern when working with Solidity. Here are a few tips for writing secure contracts:

- Use a library like OpenZeppelin for secure contract development. These libraries provide a set of tested and secure building blocks that you can use in your contracts.
- Use the Solidity static analyzer to identify potential vulnerabilities in your code.
- Follow best practices for secure contract development, such as using modifier functions and the "require" function to enforce contract logic.

Working with Large Contracts

Large contracts can be challenging to work with. Here are a few tips for working with large contracts:

- Break your contract into smaller, more manageable pieces.
- Use libraries to organize your code and make it easier to maintain.
- Use inheritance to reuse code and keep your contract size small.

Conclusion

We hope that these tips and tricks have been helpful as you work with Solidity. With these tools and techniques, you will be well on your way to becoming a proficient Solidity developer.

Exercises

To review these concepts, we will go through a series of exercises designed to test your understanding and apply what you have learned.

Write a test case for a Solidity contract that includes both positive and negative test cases.
What is the purpose of the Solidity pragma **directive?**
What is the purpose of the require() **function in Solidity?**
What is the purpose of the emit **keyword in Solidity?**
What is the purpose of the modifier **keyword in Solidity?**

Solutions

Write a test case for a Solidity contract that includes both positive and negative test cases.

```
describe("MyContract", () => {
let contract;
beforeEach(async () => {
  contract = await MyContract.new();
});
it("should return the correct value when passed a valid input", async () => {
  const result = await contract.myFunction(5);
  assert.equal(result, 10);
});
it("should throw an error when passed an invalid input", async () => {
  try {
    await contract.myFunction(-1);
  } catch (error) {
    assert.equal(error.reason, "Invalid input");
  }
});
});
```

What is the purpose of the Solidity pragma **directive?**

The pragma directive is used to specify the version of Solidity that the contract is written in, as well as any other compiler-specific options. This is useful for ensuring that the contract is compiled with the correct version of the Solidity compiler, as well as for avoiding compiler bugs and security vulnerabilities.

What is the purpose of the require() **function in Solidity?**

The require() function is used to check for conditions that must be met in order for a contract function to execute. If the condition is not met, the function will throw an exception and terminate execution. This is useful for ensuring that the contract functions are only executed under the correct conditions, and for providing a means of handling errors and exceptions in the contract.

What is the purpose of the emit **keyword in Solidity?**

The emit keyword is used to trigger an event in a Solidity contract. Events are logged entries that are stored in the contract's transaction history and can be used to trigger external functions or to provide notifications to external clients. The emit keyword allows the contract to communicate with the outside world and to provide updates on the state of the contract.

What is the purpose of the modifier **keyword in Solidity?**

The modifier keyword is used to define a reusable piece of code that can be applied to one or more contract functions. Modifiers are useful for adding common functionality to multiple functions, such as checking for permission levels or ensuring that certain conditions are met before execution. This helps to avoid duplication of code and makes it easier to maintain and update the contract.

RECAP OF THE KEY POINTS COVERED IN THE COURSE

Welcome to one of the final chapters in the "Learn Solidity" course! In this chapter, we will be reviewing the key points covered in the course and discussing some final thoughts on working with Solidity.

Solidity Basics

In the first few chapters of this course, we covered the basics of Solidity, including the history of the language, setting up a development environment, and working with variables, data types, and functions.

Smart Contracts

We then moved on to discussing smart contracts and their role in the Ethereum ecosystem. We covered the different types of smart contracts, as well as how to write and deploy them on the Ethereum network.

Advanced Solidity Features

In the following sections, we explored some of the more advanced features of Solidity, including interfaces, design patterns, and advanced data structures.

Testing and Debugging

We also emphasized the importance of testing and debugging in the Solidity development process, and provided tips and tricks for working with Oracles and real-world examples of Solidity in use.

Tips and Tricks

Finally, we shared some general tips and tricks for working with Solidity, including best practices for writing secure smart contracts and common pitfalls to avoid.

Conclusion

We hope that this course has provided a comprehensive introduction to Solidity and equipped you with the knowledge and skills needed to start building your own smart contracts. Remember to continue learning and staying up-to-date with the latest developments in the Ethereum ecosystem. Happy coding!

Exercises

To review these concepts, we will go through a series of exercises designed to test your understanding and apply what you have learned.

Write a Solidity contract that includes a public variable and a public function.
Write a Solidity contract that includes an enumeration and a function that takes in an enumeration value as a parameter.
Write a Solidity contract that includes a struct and a function that takes in a struct as a parameter.
Write a Solidity contract that includes an event and a function that triggers the event.
Write a Solidity contract that includes a mapping and a function that retrieves a value from the mapping.

Solutions

Write a Solidity contract that includes a public variable and a public function.

```solidity
pragma solidity ^0.7.0;
contract MyContract {
  uint public myVariable;
  function myFunction() public {
    myVariable = 5;
  }
}
```

Write a Solidity contract that includes an enumeration and a function that takes in an enumeration value as a parameter.

```solidity
pragma solidity ^0.7.0;
contract MyContract {
  enum MyEnum {
    Option1,
    Option2,
    Option3
  }
  function myFunction(MyEnum _enumValue) public {
    if (_enumValue == MyEnum.Option1) {
      // do something
    } else if (_enumValue == MyEnum.Option2) {
      // do something else
    } else if (_enumValue == MyEnum.Option3) {
      // do something different
    }
  }
}
```

Write a Solidity contract that includes a struct and a function that takes in a struct as a parameter.

```solidity
pragma solidity ^0.7.0;
contract MyContract {
  struct MyStruct {
    uint x;
    uint y;
  }
  function myFunction(MyStruct _struct) public {
    // do something with the struct values
    uint sum = _struct.x + _struct.y;
  }
}
```

Write a Solidity contract that includes an event and a function that triggers the event.

```solidity
pragma solidity ^0.7.0;
contract MyContract {
  event MyEvent(uint value);
  function myFunction(uint _value) public {
    emit MyEvent(_value);
  }
}
```

Write a Solidity contract that includes a mapping and a function that retrieves a value from the mapping.

```solidity
pragma solidity ^0.7.0;
contract MyContract {
  mapping(uint => uint) public myMapping;
  function myFunction(uint _key) public view returns (uint) {
    return myMapping[_key];
  }
}
```

NEXT STEPS FOR CONTINUING TO LEARN SOLIDITY

Congratulations on completing this course on Solidity! By now, you should have a strong foundation in the basics of Solidity and be well-equipped to begin writing your own smart contracts.

Next Steps

However, the journey doesn't stop here. There is always more to learn and new developments in the world of Ethereum and smart contracts. Here are some suggestions for how you can continue to improve your Solidity skills:

1. Practice, practice, practice! The best way to become proficient in any skill is to put it into practice. Try writing your own contracts, experimenting with different features and design patterns, and testing your code thoroughly.
2. Stay up to date with the latest developments in Solidity and the Ethereum ecosystem. Follow blogs and social media accounts of industry leaders and developers, attend meetups and conferences, and participate in online communities to stay in the loop.
3. Dive deeper into specific topics that interest you. There are many resources available online that cover advanced Solidity concepts, such as optimization, security, and scalability. Consider taking an advanced course or workshop to further your knowledge.
4. Contribute to the Solidity community. Whether it's by answering questions on forums, writing documentation, or contributing to open-source projects, there are many ways to give back to the community and help others learn.
5. Explore the real-world applications of Solidity. There are many projects out there that are using Solidity to solve real-world problems, from supply chain management to voting systems. Take a look at some of these projects and see how you can get involved.

Conclusion

By following these steps, you will be well on your way to becoming a proficient Solidity developer and making a meaningful impact in the world of Ethereum and smart contracts.

Exercises

To review these concepts, we will go through a series of exercises designed to test your understanding and apply what you have learned.

Write a function in Solidity that takes in two uint values and returns the larger of the two.
Write a Solidity contract that stores a list of student names and their respective grades. The contract should have a function that allows a teacher to add a new student and their grade, and a

function that allows a student to retrieve their own grade.

Write a Solidity function that takes in an array of integers and returns the sum of all the elements in the array.

Write a Solidity contract that allows a user to send ether to the contract and adds it to their balance. The contract should also have a function that allows the user to withdraw their balance.

Write a Solidity contract that allows a user to register their name and age. The contract should have a function that returns the name and age of a user given their address.

Solutions

Write a function in Solidity that takes in two uint values and returns the larger of the two.

```solidity
function largerNumber(uint x, uint y) public pure returns (uint) {
  if (x > y) {
    return x;
  } else {
    return y;
  }
}
```

Write a Solidity contract that stores a list of student names and their respective grades. The contract should have a function that allows a teacher to add a new student and their grade, and a function that allows a student to retrieve their own grade.

```solidity
pragma solidity ^0.7.0;
contract StudentGrades {
  mapping(address => uint) public grades;
  mapping(address => string) public names;
  function addStudent(string memory _name, uint _grade) public {
    require(names[msg.sender] == "", "Student already exists");
    names[msg.sender] = _name;
    grades[msg.sender] = _grade;
  }
  function getGrade(address _student) public view returns (uint) {
    return grades[_student];
  }
}
```

Write a Solidity function that takes in an array of integers and returns the sum of all the elements in the array.

```solidity
function sumArray(int[] _array) public pure returns (int _sum) {
  for (uint i = 0; i < _array.length; i++) {
```

```
    _sum += _array[i];
  }
  return _sum;
}
```

Write a Solidity contract that allows a user to send ether to the contract and adds it to their balance. The contract should also have a function that allows the user to withdraw their balance.

```solidity
pragma solidity ^0.7.0;
contract SimpleBank {
  mapping(address => uint) public balances;
  function deposit() public payable {
    balances[msg.sender] += msg.value;
  }
  function withdraw(uint _amount) public {
    require(balances[msg.sender] >= _amount, "Insufficient balance.");
    msg.sender.transfer(_amount);
    balances[msg.sender] -= _amount;
  }
}
```

Write a Solidity contract that allows a user to register their name and age. The contract should have a function that returns the name and age of a user given their address.

```solidity
pragma solidity ^0.7.0;
contract UserRegistry {
  struct User {
    string name;
    uint age;
  }
  mapping(address => User) public users;
  function registerUser(string memory _name, uint _age) public {
    users[msg.sender].name = _name;
    users[msg.sender].age = _age;
  }
  function getUser(address _address) public view returns (string memory _name, uint _age) {
    User storage user = users[_address];
    _name = user.name;
    _age = user.age;
```

```
}
```
```
}
```

THANK YOU

Thank you again for choosing "Learn Solidity". I hope it helps you in your journey to learn Solidity and achieve your goals. Please take a small portion of your time and share this with your friends and family and write a review for this book. I hope your programming journey does not end here. If you are interested, check out other books that I have or find more coding challenges at: https://codeofcode.org